D0463676

George S. Kaufman

Twayne's United States Authors Series

Kenneth E. Eble, Editor

University of Utah

TUSAS 525

GEORGE S. KAUFMAN
(1889–1961)
Courtesy of Anne Kaufman Schneider

George S. Kaufman

By Rhoda-Gale Pollack

The Wichita State University

CALVIN T. RYAN LIBRARY
KEARNEY STATE COLLEGE
KEARNEY, NEBRASKA

Twayne Publishers
A Division of G.K. Hall & Co. • *Boston*

George S. Kaufman
Rhoda-Gale Pollack

Copyright 1988 by G.K. Hall & Co.
All rights reserved.
Published by Twayne Publishers
A Division of G.K. Hall & Co.
70 Lincoln Street
Boston, Massachusetts 02111

Copyediting supervised by Lewis DeSimone
Book production by Kristina Hals
Book design by Barbara Anderson

Typeset in 11 pt. Garamond
by Compset, Inc., Beverly, MA

Printed on permanent/durable acid-free paper
and bound in the United States of America

Library of Congress Cataloging in Publication Data

Pollack, Rhoda-Gale.
  George S. Kaufman.

  (Twayne's United States authors series ; TUSAS 525)
  Bibliography: p.
  Includes index.
    1. Kaufman, George S. (George Simon), 1889–1961—
Criticism and interpretation.   I. Title.   II. Series.
PS3521.A727Z86   1988   812'.52   87-17739
ISBN 0-8057-7508-0

For two other men from Pittsburgh:
my husband, Sanford Pollack,
and
in memory of my father, Jacob A. Klein

Contents

About the Author

Rhoda-Gale Pollack received her B.F.A. from Carnegie-Mellon University, M.A. from San Francisco State University, and Ph.D. from Stanford University. She has taught in Theater Departments at the University of California-Berkeley; Mills College; San Francisco State University; and the University of Wisconsin-Parkside, where she was Coordinator of Dramatic Arts, and then Chairman of the Fine Arts Division. Presently she is Dean of the College of Fine Arts at The Wichita State University. Her professional theater credits include more than seventy productions as either director or costume designer. Her scholarly articles and reviews have appeared in *Theatre Notebook, Shakespeare Quarterly,* and *Mills Quarterly.* She has recently completed another book, *A Sampler of Plays by Women.*

Preface

George S. Kaufman worked in American theater for more than forty years. In the 1920s, during his first decade as a professional playwright, American drama began to blossom as an artistic expression worthy of recognition at home; it was also significantly interesting to warrant attention in the capitals of European culture. Kaufman and his early collaborators were innovators who molded American satirical comedy into the form that we know today. Yet, even though he is one of our country's most important playwrights his contributions to American drama have been surprisingly neglected.

Assessment of a playwright who collaborates with other writers is usually difficult. What complicates the evaluation even more in Kaufman's case is his partnership with more than a dozen different writers. Following the end of the 1930s, his name has been linked primarily to one collaborator, Moss Hart, which may be the major reason that many of the wonderful plays written with collaborators other than Hart have been neglected and even forgotten. One may readily detect that no matter with whom Kaufman collaborated, his own style is discernible: his identifiable features are marked by flashes of wit, fast-paced dialogue, jibes at potentates of business and government, volleys of wisecracks, observations on details of daily life, and an overall satiric tone.

An investigation of Kaufman's plays provides a glimpse of the evolution of American drama from 1920 to 1955, and it also furnishes a sense of the cultural, industrial, social, and political changes that took place in the United States during those three-and-a-half decades. An America in transition is reflected in his forty-five plays produced on Broadway, his more than a dozen unproduced plays, and his numerous short plays (sketches).

George S. Kaufman's other professional activities—theater director, producer, newspaper drama editor, play doctor, author of magazine and newspaper articles, and television personality—while noted in the text, are not discussed in detail. His career paths were too diverse and too filled with accomplishments to be adequately analyzed in a volume focusing on Kaufman the dramatist. The major aim of this volume is to provide an accurate and comprehensive survey of Kaufman's plays. Each phase of his career is addressed in order to provide general historical references helpful in understanding Kaufman's viewpoints; to trace the evolution of Kaufman's comedic style while trying to separate his talents from those of his collaborators; and to demonstrate that he was an innovative dramatist who was willing to experiment rather than cling to any one of his successful formulas as a means of producing a surefire Broadway sensation.

This volume is organized primarily in chronological order—presenting each of Kaufman's plays, whether full-length drama or sketch—to demonstrate the pattern of his development, the breadth of his work, the variety of his subject matter, the range of commentary he offered as a dramatist, and his prodigious productivity. Kaufman's indefatigable energies and multiple talents produced genuine accomplishments that are more evident when placed on display in the manner of a retrospective. This book is, therefore, a literary exhibition filled with information about all extant Kaufman scripts.

Every play is given nearly equal consideration in an attempt to determine plot, patterns of style, general themes, and specific nuances. Another reason for including exposure to all plays is that it is difficult to gain access to every script: Many Kaufman plays are no longer available in either book form or acting script; other plays exist only in manuscript form and are scattered around the country in theater collections at various libraries. Many of the original manuscripts are typed on paper that is becoming increasingly fragile and disintegrating owing to age.

The approach in addressing the question of Kaufman's critical acceptance has been to provide a sample of reviews available for every play that opened on Broadway. Some of the critical and scholarly opinions about Kaufman's works are also included to offer the reader an indication of how a particular play and the playwright's works, in general, have been regarded from one era to another. Many of Kaufman's plays are relatively unknown today because writers of comedy are often given less long-range critical attention than playwrights who create serious dramas. Comedies, particularly those with satirical tone, tend to be topical; therefore, as the subject loses its relevance, the importance of the play fades. With this in mind, it is enlightening to see how many of the Kaufman's satirical comedies are still entertaining theater pieces in our time.

Currently there is a growing appreciation for several of Kaufman's plays, and theaters all over the world are staging revivals of these works. Plays such as *The Royal Family, Merton of the Movies, Once in a*

Lifetime, and *June Moon* are joining the ever-popular Kaufman classics—*The Man Who Came to Dinner, The Solid Gold Cadillac,* and *You Can't Take It with You*—that are regularly staged. Audiences experiencing Kaufman's plays have the opportunity to understand the light his humor brought to America during those earlier twentieth-century decades of depression, sorrow, and prosperity.

Rhoda-Gale Pollack

The Wichita State University

Acknowledgments

To Anne Kaufman Schneider, whose kindness and assistance throughout the research and writing stages of this project were indispensable.

To the following individuals who contributed invaluable assistance: Emily and Roger Hill; Sandy Puzerewski; Alan R. Schucard; Mary Elizabeth Shutler.

To the following library staffs I extend my appreciation for their willing and expert assistance: University of Wisconsin-Parkside and B.J. Nelson and Judith M. Pryor in particular; the Library of Congress and Mike Dwyer; Billy Rose Collection of the New York Public Library at Lincoln Center; Louis A. Rachow of The Walter Hampden-Edwin Booth Theatre Collection at The Players Club, New York; the William Seymour Theatre Collection at Princeton University; The Institute of Jazz Studies at Rutgers University and Dan Morgenstern; and the Wisconsin Center for Film and Theatre Research at the Wisconsin Historical Society in Madison.

To Cecily Ruth Ulrich-Gaura, to whom I am particularly indebted for her scrutiny of every chapter of the manuscript.

To the Committee on Research and Creative Activity at the University of Wisconsin-Parkside, which helped to finance portions of the research travel.

To the National Endowment for the Humanities for a Travel to the Collections Grant, which enabled me to do my research work at the Library of Congress.

Chronology

1889   George S. Kaufman born 16 November in Pittsburgh, Pennsylvania, the third child of Joseph Kaufman and Henrietta Myers Kaufman.

1907   Graduates from Pittsburgh Central High, where he had the opportunity to participate in a school play and write for the school publications.

1909   The Kaufman family moves to New Jersey. George remains in Pittsburgh.

1910   Moves to Passaic, New Jersey. Works as a ribbon salesman. Enrolls in the Alveine School of Dramatic Art in New York City for a weekly class.

1911   Reworks first play, "The Failure," started in 1903 with his boyhood friend, Irving Pichel; play never produced.

1912   Moves to Washington, D.C. to begin writing a newspaper column titled "This and That with Sometimes a Little of the Other" for the *Washington Times*.

1913   Returns to New York City where his parents now reside; begins working as a reporter for the *New York Tribune*.

1914   Writes "The Lunatic" with Herbert Seligman, a friend; play never produced.

1917   Marries Beatrice Bakrow on 15 March; in September leaves the *Tribune* to work as drama editor on the *New York Times*.

1918   "Someone in the House," first produced play opens in New York on 9 September.

1919   Meets Marc Connelly on 5 May.

1921   *Dulcy* written with Connelly, first Broadway success.

1922   *To the Ladies!*, "West of Pittsburgh," and *Merton of the Movies* written with Connelly.

1923   "Helen of Troy, New York"—first musical by Connelly and Kaufman.

1924   *Beggar on Horseback,* a play; and "Be Yourself," a musical; both written with Connelly. *Minick* written with Edna Ferber.

1925   *Butter and Egg Man,* a play; and *The Cocoanuts,* a musical, written without a collaborator for the Marx Brothers. Beatrice and George adopt a baby girl named Anne.

1927   *The Royal Family* written with Ferber; it became the longest running play Kaufman had worked on to date.

1928   Begins stage-director career that will span thirty years; stages *The Front Page,* which opens 14 August.

1929   *Animal Crackers,* another musical written for the Marx Brothers; book collaborator: Morrie Ryskind, lyrics and music by Bert Kalmar and Harry Ruby.

1930   *Once in a Lifetime* marks the beginning of collaboration with Moss Hart. Resigns his post at the *New York Times.*

1931   *Of Thee I Sing,* first musical to win a Pulitzer Prize; book written with Ryskind, music by George Gershwin, and lyrics by Ira Gershwin.

1932   *Dinner at Eight* written with Ferber; opens in New York 22 October, and in London at the end of the year.

1933   *Dark Tower,* written with Alexander Woollcott, published by Random House following its Broadway debut; one of the first dramatic texts to be published by the firm that would issue most of Kaufman's subsequent scripts. Samuel Goldwyn lures Kaufman to Hollywood to write a screenplay for Eddie Cantor. Kaufman and his cowriter Robert E. Sherwood eventually withdraw from the production.

1936   *Stage Door,* written with Ferber, opens 22 October; *You Can't Take It with You,* written with Moss Hart, opens 14 December. The latter play wins Pulitzer Prize and runs for 837 performances.

1939   *The Man Who Came to Dinner,* written in collaboration with Hart, another major success.

1940   *George Washington Slept Here,* written with Hart, opens 18 October.

1944   *The Late George Apley,* coauthored with John P. Marquand, opens for a successful run 21 November.

1945   Beatrice Kaufman dies 6 October.

1949   26 May marries Leueen MacGrath, a British actress. Begins to serve as a weekly panelist on the television program "This Is Show Business."

1950   Begins writing scripts with Leueen MacGrath.

1951   Suffers a stroke in October prior to starting rehearsals for *Fancy Meeting You Again.*

1953   Illness plagues Kaufman early in the year while working on *The Solid Gold Cadillac.* This play, written with Howard Teichmann, opens 5 November.

1955   *Silk Stockings,* book written with MacGrath and doctored by Abe Burrows, score by Cole Porter, opens in February; Kaufman suffers another stroke while play is in rehearsal.

1956–1961   Works with Alan Campbell, Ruth Goetz, Connelly, MacGrath, and Teichmann on scripts that were either never produced or never completed.

1957   Divorced by Leueen MacGrath in August.

1961   Dies 2 June.

Chapter One
The Years of Exploring

George S. Kaufman, who many Americans invited into their homes weekly in the early 1950s by turning the television dial to "This Is Show Business," was regarded as a master of humor. His rapid-fire witticisms, often sharpened with satirical flourish, tickled, charmed, and sometimes angered a large public. For more than forty years during his lifetime he entertained with magazine articles, newspaper columns, and plays. His story of success is based on a young man going east rather than following the famous nineteenth-century dictum—"Go west, young man."

Pittsburgh

The Kaufman side of the family had settled in Pittsburgh, Pennsylvania, in the late 1840s after immigrating from Germany.[1] Grandfather Simon eventually prospered in his new country as a manufacturer of trousers. His son Joseph, one of ten children, married Henrietta (Nettie) Myers, a second cousin, on 17 January 1884. George was born to Joseph and Nettie on 16 November 1889. He was the third-born of four children, but the death of his brother preceded George's birth by at least a year. As the only son, George was overprotected by his mother, thereby allowing him hours of freedom to pursue his own interest, which included reading and writing. George often spent pleasurable sessions reading Mark Twain, and his enthusiasm for the earlier humorist remained throughout his lifetime.

George's interest in theater also developed during his adolescence. He joined a dramatic society organized by Rabbi J. Leonard Levy, who served at the Rodef Shalom Temple. Rabbi Levy believed George possessed a talent for acting, and the clergyman urged the family to encourage the youth in a stage career. In addition to his dramatics activities with the society, George saw plays presented in Pittsburgh by touring and stock companies. In 1903, when George was only fourteen, he and his friend Irving Pichel began writing a play, "The Failure." Eight years later it provided the framework for his first dramatic script, which Kaufman entered for copyright at the Library of Congress.

Upon graduation from Pittsburgh Central High in 1907, George selected neither a theatrical nor a writing career. He chose to enter law school at Western University of Pennsylvania, which was by the end of the year renamed the University of Pittsburgh. During the first semester pleurisy disrupted his studies and George withdrew from the university. This must have been a major disappointment for Joseph Kaufman, who had managed to save money for George's education during periods of successful business ventures and who protected the funds when the failure of his company forced him to move from job to job.

George started to follow his nomadic father's job pattern. The lanky, six-foot, untrained youth began as a member of a surveying team, switched to public payroll clerk in the Allegheny County tax office, and then the controller's stenographer at the Pittsburgh Coal Company. In 1909, when Joseph Kaufman was given the opportunity to manage the Columbia Ribbon Mill in Patterson, New Jersey, the family moved from Pittsburgh. George remained in Pittsburgh until his father provided him with a job as a salesman of Columbia Ribbon products, but this was not the type of position best suited for George, who at twenty was introverted and shy.

Passaic

When he was twenty, George joined his family, who had recently moved into a rented house in Passaic, New Jersey. He spent three years as a salesman while gaining informal journalistic experience. George wrote light verses and bits of humor that were accepted for publication by the local newspaper. Seeing his work in print gave George the courage to send similar pieces to a daily column titled "Always in Good Humor."

This column appeared in the *New York Evening Mail*; it was written and edited by Franklin Pierce Adams, a popular writer more commonly recognized by his initials (F.P.A.). At the time, it was common practice for readers to submit unsolicited material that columnists would print, and Adams began to use Kaufman's contributions regularly. Curiosity eventually led Adams to invite his youthful contributor to lunch. Their first meeting marked the beginning of a lifelong friendship.

Adams became Kaufman's role model and mentor. In many ways the younger man absorbed the style used by Adams, including the use of a middle initial in his name for his byline. Kaufman decided on the initial S, which in later years he would say stood for Simon, in honor of his paternal grandfather.

In addition to being a regular contributor to Adam's column, Kaufman began in 1910, at his mentor's suggestion, to think about becoming an actor. He enrolled in the Alveine School of Dramatic Art in New York City and attended class once a week. His passion for the theater was rekindled. Kaufman and Irving Pichel—then a student at Harvard College, who would become an actor and film director—decided to rework their boyhood manuscript, "The Failure." The play was expanded into three acts, rewritten extensively, and polished. The title was retained since it refers to the protagonist, Radigasius Jones, Ph.D., an academic at Wharton College located near New York City.

In "The Failure" Professor Jones has sacrificed his own scholarly achievements for the past ten years in order to finance the educations of his daughter Rene, a promising pianist, and his ward, Walter Randolph, an artist who believes his current portrait will win the major competition he has entered. Act 1 is filled with expectations of success for Professor Jones and his ward. Act 2 brims with frustration and rage that are the result of the professor's self-sacrificing behavior. Jones loses his opportunity to become president of the college because he has never finished his book on Egypt. Walter demands that Jones divulge the details of his late father's estate, which the elder man keeps from him. Walter also claims he will marry the professor's daughter without permission.

Professor Jones is hurt by his failure to be named president, but he becomes more devastated by the prospects of losing his daughter and the rewards of success she would have gained for them both as an acclaimed concert pianist. (If she marries Walter, she could not as a married woman have a public career.) In a moment of uncontrolled emotion Jones destroys the portrait and with it Walter's hopes of immediate recognition and financial gain.

Act 3 forces the theme and produces a reconciliation of sorts. The philosophy of Professor Jones is stated in his lines: "That's what is the true success—to find purpose, and work towards it. It doesn't matter so much if you don't get there. . . ." The daughter arrives home to share her good news with her father about a series of concert engagements she has been offered. She reaffirms her father's values regarding purpose and sacrifice. The sour note is Walter. The recalcitrant remains unforgiving in spite of his new awareness that Professor Jones had paid for his education out of his own earnings because the estate lacked the funds. However, one is left with the feeling that Rene will lead Walter to see the error of his blindness. The point is made that Jones is not a failure with a daughter like Rene. Also, some of his former students arrive to attest to the fact that Jones had instilled purpose into their lives. In a final gesture of satisfaction and release from his bond to Walter, Professor Jones returns to his Egyptian research project with vigor and purpose.

The reworked version of "The Failure" seems to be influenced by the social comedy written by Clyde Fitch, whose dramas were originally produced from 1890 to 1910. Fitch, remembered primarily for *The Girl with the Green Eyes* (1902) and *The Truth* (1906), focused on details ignored in American drama prior to his works. He desired to present an accurate sense of some aspect of American life, to illustrate the relationship between society and individual human beings, and to establish inherent weaknesses in the personalities of the two central characters.[2] These traits are utilized in varying degrees by Pichel and Kaufman, since they provide glimpses into the working of college politics; they clearly establish clues as to how Professor Jones is regarded by both supporters and detractors; and they blatantly reveal personal blindnesses of Professor Jones and Walter.

Another distinctive feature of "The Failure" is the role of the professor's daughter, Rene. She has received an extraordinary musical education for a woman. Her father believed in her ability and provided her with the best instruction. She in turn does not toss away her career opportunities to marry Walter. Rene appears to be an intelligent woman who will survive as an artist in a social milieu that places barriers before talented women. She seems to spring from portraits of artists as new women created by playwright Rachel Crothers, who had been following the advance currents of social-problem plays since 1908. Two plays by Crothers, *Myself Bettina* staged in 1908 and *A Man's World* produced in 1910, could have provided character models for Rene.

"The Failure" was never produced, and whether Pichel and Kaufman even tried to attract a producer is dubious. The surviving copy of the manuscript in the Library of Congress has the third act written in longhand rather than typed. In other words, the manuscript does not appear to have been prepared for professional scrutiny.

In 1912 Kaufman's career took another turn. Columnist Adams recommended his protégé to be the writer and editor of a humor column with the *Washington Times*.

Washington, a Brief Interlude

Kaufman moved to Washington in the fall of 1912, and began his daily column with the 9 December issue. The column titled "This and That with Sometimes a Little of the Other" provided Kaufman with a starting salary of twenty dollars per week. For the young journalist, who lacked formal training, creating a daily column filled with humorous commentary on social and political events as well as supplying a steady dose of verse was obviously a demanding situation. Kaufman quickly began to demonstrate his skills at satirizing big business, class-consciousness, and political institutions. These talents would be honed to perfection over the remaining years of his life and used repeatedly.

During 1913 Joseph, Nettie, and their younger daughter Ruth moved to Manhattan. Joseph left Columbia Ribbon and purchased his own small business, the New York Silk Dyeing Company. This move to New York City would be a comfort to George in the waning weeks of 1913, since his employment at the *Washington Times* came to an abrupt end after one year.

The owner of the newspaper, Frank A. Munsey, did not hire Jewish writers. For some reason he had failed to interview Kaufman, and he never saw him until a year after the columnist's arrival. Reportedly, Munsey upon seeing Kaufman in the city room asked who he might be. When Kaufman's identity was revealed, Munsey was enraged over the breach in his hiring policy. There are several varying accounts of this incident in print.[3] Kaufman was dismissed. He returned to his family and their new home in Manhattan.

New York City

Within two months of Kaufman's move to New York, Adams helped to get him a job as a cub reporter covering minor news events on the *New York Tribune*. Since Adams had recently moved his daily column to this prestigious publication, he was able to acquire the apprentice-ship position for Kaufman.

Other new writing opportunities awaited Kaufman in 1914. He col-laborated on a one-act play with a new acquaintance named Herbert Seligman.[4] The comedy, titled "The Lunatic," is set in the reception room of the Luna Private Sanitarium, Limited.

John Winters, the only patient in the sanitarium, was not there due to mental illness. He had bet his friend James Kennedy that he would convince his family of the need to institutionalize him. Now that Win-ters has succeeded in this game, he tries to explain the situation to Dr. Kelly and the beautiful Nurse Burdick. They refuse to believe him since the sanitarium is heavily in debt, and they need the money paid by the Winters family. The fragile plot moves ahead after Kennedy arrives at the sanitarium to save his friend, and the complication arises when Kennedy falls in love with Burdick at first sight. Kennedy acts in an irrational manner so that he can be admitted to the mental facil-ity. Once patient status is established for Kennedy, both young men are told that they can obtain their releases if they buy the debt-ridden establishment for $40,000. The patients write their checks for the pur-chase of the sanitarium, believing Nurse Burdick will remain on the staff. Both Winters and Kennedy immediately propose marriage to the nurse, but she informs them that she and Dr. Kelly are engaged. Nurse Burdick thanks her admirers for the checks and informs them that their monies are lovely wedding presents.

The play has several comic moments in which quackery is ridiculed. This first attempt by Kaufman at comedy for the stage can still provoke a few laughs. The play was not produced, but it provided its authors with an opportunity to work on the simplified, limited plot construc-tion of the one-act form.

In 1914 Kaufman also planned another venture with Herbert Selig-man. They decided to take a five-week trip to Europe with the depar-ture date set for 3 July. Kaufman returned to the United States only one week before the first shots of World War I were fired. He took up his position again at the *Tribune,* but this time he was assigned feature articles for which he was credited with a byline.

Adams, once again, encouraged Kaufman to do something toward learning more about the theater. Kaufman enrolled in an extension course in playwriting offered one night a week at Columbia University. In addition to writing original scripts, the course included visits to the theater followed by classroom discussions analyzing the production.[5]

The course was taught by Hatcher Hughes, who in 1924 would receive the Pulitzer Prize for *Hell-Bent fer Heaven*. Hughes taught the essential characteristics of the well-made play: clear exposition of situation; unexpected but logical reversals; careful preparation for future events; continuous and mounting suspense; an obligatory scene showing the moment toward which the play has been heading to test the success or failure of the action; and a logical and believable resolution. Kaufman utilized some of the techniques learned in this course, but he never became a slave to this formula, which was in disfavor in Europe with such innovators as Henrik Ibsen and George Bernard Shaw.

A play that may have been a product of this course and written with another Columbia student, W. W. De Renne, is titled "That Infernal Machine."[6] The authors apparently tried using some of the techniques they learned during the semester, especially the unexpected but logical reversal. The plot is built on the one-joke sketch formula popular at that time. A shy businessman, James Walker, is in love with his stenographer, Edith Roberts, but he lacks the courage to complete his proposal speech to Edith. Robert Butler, a friend of Walker's, brings him a dictation machine and persuades Walker to record a proposal message for Edith. However, when the stenographer comes into the office for the machine and leaves with it, she drops the record, which breaks. Edith then confesses that she had asked Butler to aid her in obtaining the trick proposal. Walker gains courage during that moment of truth and proposes to Edith face to face. The play ends on a note of impending nuptial bliss.

This script offers a glimpse into the style that would eventually bring acclaim for Kaufman as a playwright. The seeds of his comedic style are discernible in the dialogue, which is fast-paced and filled with repartee.

Another distinctive Kaufman attribute is evident in "That Infernal Machine": the playwright as social historian. In this play a piece of new office equipment humorously illustrates the changes one invention could evoke. Subsequent plays by Kaufman and his collaborators also offer ideas of what was fashionable at the time—of what plays, songs, books, or persons were the most popular; of the topics most discussed; of new inventions or gadgets that changed everyday manners; and of the latest in motion-picture madness. Kaufman not only exposed these superficial aspects of American daily existence, but he would gain a reputation for delineating topics that dealt fundamentally with the laws and practices of business, politics, and society.

Other breakthroughs were to occur for Kaufman in 1915. After Adams left the *Evening Mail* in 1914, the newspaper began seeking a suitable replacement to write the daily humor column. Eventually the editor requested advice from Adams and Kaufman was recommended. Kaufman's first column for the *Evening Mail* was published on 15 February 1915. His service was brief, however, because a syndicate buyout of the publication resulted in a change of editorial philosophy. By late July of the same year, Kaufman was back at the *Tribune* and assigned as a reporter to the drama department headed by Heywood Broun, the principal reviewer. Kaufman's job was to gather news from producers' offices for a Sunday feature article. The bonus associated with this chore was complimentary tickets to Broadway productions.

In the fall of 1915 Kaufman enrolled in another extension course at Columbia. The subject was modern drama from Victor Hugo to Arthur Wing Pinero—obviously a conventional approach to the topic since Pinero was one of the traditional playwrights of the era. These extension courses—coupled with his newly acquired opportunity to see many Broadway productions—provided him with invaluable theater training. He was learning new critical skills in the classroom and applying them to the best theatrical productions offered in the United States. Thus the career pieces that would eventually come together for Kaufman were at last taking shape.

Kaufman undertook his next playwriting enterprise alone, "Going Up," a farce in three acts with prologue. The main thread of the plot exposes the criminal practice of check-raising—increasing the monetary value of the check after it has passed from the hands of the payer. Sam Blaine, a writer, receives a check for eight dollars from Gotham Publishing for a poem that the company plans to print. Blaine is persuaded by Robert ("Skin") Flint to raise the check to eighty dollars before giving it to his landlady Mrs. Rose Gersten for back rent. Mrs. Gersten also falls under Flint's influence, and she raises the check to eight hundred dollars in order to pay her back payments on the boarding house. This farce slowly but merrily moves forward until three detectives detain all the culprits who participated in raising the eight-dollar check to eight thousand. Woven into the situation is a secondary confidence game connected to the stock market. Several of the characters are trying to cash in on a stock market tip, an' a running joke revolves around inquiries into the stock's current se.ling price. The denouement reveals that Flint had covered the check-raising he had encouraged because he was trying to prove to Mr. Runyon, Manager of Gotham Publishing Corporation, that his company needed to purchase a check-protecting machine. Meanwhile the stock, which has inched downward throughout the plot, makes an incredible comeback in the final moments, and all the investors become wealthy. There is also a romantic subplot—involving Blaine and Helen Parker, a stenographer at Gotham—which ends happily.

In "Going Up" Kaufman continued to experiment with plot devices. The action relies on the use of two reversals in order to resolve the situations. In this work Kaufman also used a relatively new theatrical technique—the flashback. The prologue takes place in the office of Gotham Publishing Corporation twenty-four hours after the events staged in act 1, thereby making the first act a flashback. This is a narrative device that would become commonplace by the late 1920s; it is a cinematic technique used occasionally in the silent films, and adapted to the theater by Elmer Rice in his successful play *On Trial* staged in 1914.

"Going Up" also examines specified business practices in a witty, sparkling manner. The play has charm and humor even though the characters are thinly drawn and the story drags at times. This script was submitted to Henry R. Stern, who was forming an agency for new playwrights. He liked the play but never found a producer for it. However, the script was read by George C. Tyler, a prominent producer, who did not care to mount the play, but was impressed enough with the dramatist's ability to keep Kaufman in mind for future projects.

The Ides of March, 1917, marks the day George S. Kaufman married Beatrice Bakrow, an intelligent, amusing young woman six years his junior. Their meeting had been arranged in July 1916 by Kaufman's younger sister Ruth when George was on a vacation with Ruth and her husband in Rochester, New York. On 2 April 1917, when the United States entered World War I, the newlyweds were setting up their first apartment. Kaufman was not inducted into the armed services because of poor eyesight and other physical frailties. In early September the couple was settling into the routines of married life when Kaufman assumed the position of drama editor on the *New York Times*. It was a post that he would hold until 1930.

Kaufman's next assignment as a playwright came from producer George C. Tyler, who had previously commissioned author Larry Evans and actor Walter C. Percival to adapt two short stories by Evans into a play. When the production of "Among Those Present" had its out-of-town tryouts, the reviews were poor. Tyler remained committed to the project, however, so he asked Kaufman to serve as a rewrite man. Although Kaufman was neither the first nor the last person to serve as "play doctor" on this script, his revisions were so extensive—particularly those related to the characters of Helene Glendenning played by Lynn Fontanne and Percy Glendenning played by Hassard Short—that George S. Kaufman's name was added to the program credits.

In this play that Kaufman tried to refashion, Jimmy Burke, a jewel thief known as "The Dancer," is a gentleman crook, who plans to steal the famous Hollister diamond necklace. The gems have not been worn in public for years, but the necklace is scheduled to be worn in an amateur theatrical presentation staged by members of the Westchester Hill Society for the Field Hospital Fund. Jimmy Burke managed to get cast as the leading man for the play written by Percy Glendenning, staged by him, and rehearsed in his country home. Acts 2 and 3 are filled with bits of rehearsals, suspicions about Jimmy, and sensational publicity stunts focusing on the necklace.

In act 3 the arrival of celebrated New York City detective Peter B. Halloran complicates all aspects of the story. Act 4 builds toward the moment of discovery when the valuable necklace is thought to be missing and Jimmy Burke (whose identity as "The Dancer" has just been revealed) has secretly left the house. This story follows the pattern of the popular "Crook-play" of the period. It allows the dashing, clever criminal to win the sympathy of the audience, who is delighted when he eludes capture by the police for past offenses, but is slightly disappointed when he ducks out of the life of the ingenue, who has lost her heart to him. (The gentleman crook could never marry the lovely lady since his enjoyment of his trade makes him seem beyond reform.)

Even though Kaufman did not turn this opus into a hit, Tyler determinedly pursued opening the production on Broadway the night of 9 September 1918. For some reason Tyler thought a title change would enhance the play's chances: "Someone in the House" opened to modest reviews and ran for thirty-two performances. Reviewers lauded Lynn Fontanne's performance in the role Kaufman had created for her. The review dated 10 September 1918, in the *New York Times* states that the comedy is introduced in the second act and that it never departs. It goes on to mention that Fontanne and Short "have lines with which to make the most of their talents at appearing as human absurdities and one gets the habit of laughing at everything they say and do."

Fontanne, who had arrived in the United States in 1916 from England, was under contract to Tyler and was the protégée of his wife, actress Laurette Taylor. It was important to Tyler that Fontanne be successful in "Someone in the House." So despite the fact that Kaufman's debut as a Broadway playwright was not a stellar event, it provided him with a launching pad and George C. Tyler's goodwill.

While "Someone in the House" was going through its many drafts, Kaufman also collaborated on "Third Man High" with Robert Nathan, who was married to Beatrice Kaufman's best friend Dorothy. Nathan would in the succeeding years earn a reputation as a novelist (primarily), poet, and playwright. He divorced Dorothy in 1922, and Kaufman never collaborated with him again.

"Third Man High," labeled a political farce by its authors, is set in a city in the Middle West. The protagonist—Peter Jamison,[7] a reporter out of work—accidentally lands a job as valet for James Ryan, a political boss. Peter persuades Ryan to hire Janet Wilson, another tenant who lives in the same boarding house, to become the politico's private stenographer. In act 1 set a month later Peter and Janet are established in their new positions. Ryan is preoccupied with the Democratic convention being held nearby. He is trying to get his candidate nominated for governor, but his man begins to lose support even before the nominating speeches are made. In an attempt to save his candidate, Ryan decides to run a dud in order to divide the votes of the opposition. His random choice for the diversionist is his valet Peter, who succeeds in winning the party's nomination, but, of course, loses Ryan's patronage.

Six weeks later the Jamison campaign is running like clockwork when trouble begins to gather on the horizon. The campaign committee plans a meeting to discuss the handling of funds. Jamison could be in trouble because he is using some campaign funds for living expenses. Ryan, who has lost control of the Democratic party, tries to get Jamison to join forces with him. The candidate, who is really an honest person, figures out a winning solution for himself and divines how to achieve clean state politics. Upon resigning his candidacy, Jamison endorses the Republican candidate. Jamison has accepted a position as head of advertising for a New York film company at a very impressive annual salary of seventy thousand dollars. He and Janet, who has been working with him on the campaign, declare their love for each other and plan to live happily ever after in New York.

This play is not as well constructed as "Going Up." It rambles particularly in the third act, since the characters become less interesting as the plot progresses, and the reversals are fairly numerous and sometimes too predictable. Most notably, this play's main weakness foreshadows a problem that Kaufman repeats in future works. The first act shows promise, but in the remaining acts the plot and sometimes the characters are sacrificed to fast-paced, witty dialogue and forced actions. "Going Up" was never produced.

The final months of 1918 became a difficult time for the Kaufmans, who had eagerly awaited the birth of their baby. The infant was still-born in November and complications from the birth deprived Beatrice of ever again being able to conceive. The couple attempted to adjust to this double disappointment. Supposedly, for the remainder of their married life, they also had to cope with problems that affected their physical relationship. Beatrice went to work as an assistant to the press agent of Norma and Constance Talmadge, two extremely popular actresses of the silent screen. George buried himself in his writing projects.

In 1919 George Tyler provided Kaufman with an assignment involving a script by the Danish dramatist Hans Miller.[8] Tyler purchased the American rights after the play had a successful European production, and he wanted Kaufman to adapt the script. Tyler changed the working title of "Duval, M.D." to "Jacques Duval" before the play opened its out-of-town performances in Chicago's Blackstone Theatre on 10 November 1919.

This gloomy melodrama centers around a physician, Jacques Duval, who has lost his concern for human beings. He is interested solely in his scientific experiments and achievements as a means of defeating nature. His philosophy is based on Napoleon's statement that men are nothing, man is everything. As a result of being obsessed by his research, Duval neglects his marital obligations and drives his young wife Marie to seek companionship with another man. Marie has befriended an aristocratic gentleman named Marquis de Charvet. The marquis is suffering from tuberculosis; he eventually requests Duval to treat his ailment. Duval realizes the marquis is extremely ill and attempts to cure his patient with an experimental medicine from his laboratory. Charvet dies, and Duval's conduct is reviewed by the Council of Ethics composed of faculty from the local medical university. Rather than destroy the research work being conducted in his laboratory, Duval desires that the council believe he deliberately poisoned the marquis because of Marie's relationship to the patient. During the resolution of the plot Marie produces a suicide note she received from the marquis revealing that he deliberately had taken an overdose of heroin to end his life. As a result of the situation, Duval regains his humanity, is reunited with Marie, and is granted the right to continue his research.

Kaufman was given credit as the adapter of the script, but the original author was unmentioned. The reviewer for *Variety* commented, "As for the script, George S. Kauffman [sic] did a good, clean job of playwriting in the adaption . . . but he was helpless in his efforts to introduce through the heavy tone of ether and iodoform which permeates the play one single breath of natural fresh air."[9] This commentary was kind, considering Kaufman was totally out of his element on this drama. It was a play without any wit, set in a foreign locale where Kaufman—the social historian—was a stranger, and burdened with a wordy style reminiscent of late nineteenth-century scripts. The production moved on to several other cities on the tryout circuit, but closed in Boston.

Although this "Jacques Duval" project was a failure, other 1918 events may have served as positive distractions from any symptoms of melancholia Kaufman may have harbored. World War I had been concluded, and the service men who had fought in the war to end all wars were returning home. Among them were Kaufman's friends and colleagues whose literary endeavors would eventually establish a cultural recognition for the United States. It was a time of hope, new ideas, and different expectations.

One of Kaufman's colleagues, who was filled with the desire to celebrate his return to civilian life was Alexander Woollcott—theater critic for the *New York Times*. He decided to hold a festive luncheon at the Algonquin Hotel at 59 West 44th Street. Even though the Algonquin dated back to 1902, it was not until this time that it became the regular gathering place for many congenial writers and theater people.[10] George and Beatrice Kaufman were early members of the informal group as was John Peter Toohey—Tyler's press agent who introduced Woollcott to the Algonquin. Other regulars were Franklin P. Adams; Heywood and Ruth Hale Broun; Dorothy Parker; Robert E. Sherwood; Robert Benchley; Laurence Stallings; Deems Taylor; Edna Ferber; Herman J. Mankiewicz; Margaret Leech; actress Peggy Wood and her husband, John V. A. Weaver; actress Margalo Gillmore; Arthur Samuels; William Murray; Brock and Murdock Pemberton; Harold Ross and his wife, Janet Grant; Neysa McMein; and Marc Connelly.

In addition to this group, there were over the ten years of lunchtime meetings the occasional guests who were readily accepted: Ring

Lardner, Morrie Ryskind, Ina Claire, Frank Sullivan, Harpo Marx, and Donald Ogden Stewart. The attributes required for entrance into the coterie were wit and ability to evoke it in others and the common sense not to try to dominate the conversation. Money, fame, and/or talent never were considered necessary in order to be given an invitation to join the Vicious Circle, the name the members gave themselves after owner/manager Frank Case began seating them at a round table. Outsiders referred to them either as the Algonquin Round Table or the Algonquin Wits because many of the members became major contributors to the Golden Age of American Humor. The early twenties marked the peak of comic writing in the United States, when satire, parody, and sheer nonsense were created for one purpose—to be funny. This age that ushered in the time of laughter found its wits at the Algonquin. George S. Kaufman chose his collaborators for the new decade from the membership of the group as the youthful participants eagerly advanced into the 1920s.

Chapter Two
Enter Marc Connelly

Prior to the time of the Algonquin gatherings, George S. Kaufman and Marc Connelly saw each other frequently, for they attended the same plays and made the same rounds to producers' offices. When they finally spoke to each other in the spring of 1919, each had one Broadway credit—Kaufman's 1918 "Someone in the House" and Connelly's 1918 fifteen-performance run of "The Amber Princess"—and desired more.[1]

A friendship developed between the two aspiring playwrights who shared a number of common traits. Both hailed from western Pennsylvania—Connelly was born on 13 December 1890, in McKeesport located approximately fifteen miles southeast of Pittsburgh. Both shared fathers with the first name of Joseph, a love of theater, and journalism as a trade—Connelly was a reporter for the *Morning Telegraph* when they met. Connelly recalls in his autobiography *Voices Offstage* that "night after night, after our papers went to press, George and I walk uptown with each other, discussing ideas that might be dramatic material."[2]

First Successes

In the fall of 1929 producer George C. Tyler asked Kaufman to write a play for Lynn Fontanne that would feature a character like Helene Glendenning from "Someone in the House." Kaufman requested Connelly's collaboration on the project and Tyler finally agreed.

Helene Glendenning had been inspired by a fictional character who turned up regularly in "The Conning Tower," the column written by Franklin P. Adams. She was a suburban housewife who spouted bromides: "It never rains if you have your umbrella" or "When you need a policeman you can never find one." These frequently uttered banal statements could have been maddening during the course of a performance if the character had not been created as an attractive young woman. Adams had given his creature the name of Dulcinea. Kaufman and Connelly shortened the name to Dulcy and proceeded to embellish their lady with eccentric impulses. The playwrights acknowledged their debt to Adams by giving him ten percent of their profits and stating "With a Bow to Franklin P. Adams" after their names in the published script.

Connelly comments on the process they used for their first endeavor: "Quickly the characters, their development, and the narrative progression were sketched in great detail. Within a few days we had a completely articulated synopsis of about twenty-five pages. We then individually chose scenes for which we had predilections, wrote drafts, and then went over them together for improvement. Sometimes each would like the others' writing of a scene enough to let it stand for the final draft, but most passages were the result of considerable rewriting." Connelly further elaborates on this first effort: "George's wit sparkled on everything we did. The only areas in our plays which he shied from were love scenes."[3] They finished *Dulcy* in less than a month.

Dulcinea "Dulcy" Smith is the central force of *Dulcy,* and the story line unfolds as a result of her antics. She arranges a social weekend at the Smiths' Westchester home for her husband's future business partner Mr. Forbes, his wife, and daughter. Dulcy's goal is to get Mr. Forbes to offer her husband, Gordon, a more favorable percentage of the pearl manufacturing business that Smith hopes to merge with the costume jewelry company owned by Forbes. Dulcy's assemblage of persons selected to win favor with the business tycoon continuously fails in its mission. She invites a motion picture scenarist who is in love with Miss Forbes and whom Forbes dislikes; a supposedly wealthy society gentleman who enters into a flirtation with Mrs. Forbes; and her brother Bill Parker who is also in love with the alluring daughter. Uninvited, but attending the gathering nevertheless, is an advertising man who works for Forbes. He is another young man smitten by Miss Forbes. In addition, a butler who has been hired for the weekend is an ex-convict whom Dulcy hopes to rehabilitate.

Toward the conclusion of act 2 the situations arising from this group greatly agitate magnate Forbes, and consequently he desires to return to New York. But by this time there are several complications in the plot that prevent Mr. Forbes from departing. In act 3 the dilemmas of the previous evening are resolved. So despite Dulcy's meddlesome intrusions into Gordon's business deal, she achieves her goal of assisting him to secure a better future.

Dulcy opened successfully in Chicago 20 February 1921, at the Cort Theater, where it stayed for many months. The New York opening was on 13 August, and it became one of the few Broadway offerings of the season that was sold out every night. In the October 1921 *Theatre Arts* magazine the reviewer raved that *Dulcy* was "clean, wholesome and jolly, knit together with a nice sense of cumulative interest, peppered with dialogue, salient with native, naive wit." This person believes *Dulcy* is as good as *Clarence,* a 1919 comedy of youth written by Booth Tarkington. "These two plays are really reflexes of our American spirit and deserve permanent places in the repertoire of the native drama," concludes the reviewer.

This Kaufman and Connelly play was praised in all quarters for being sharp, witty, and truly satirical. (It seems that most other plays passing for satire usually were thin on wit and theme.) Kaufman and Connelly were applauded for their ridicule of the infant motion picture and advertising industries. While other playwrights had also begun to use business deals and advertising for comedic effect, in *Dulcy* Kaufman and Connelly introduced new, sophisticated, verbal thrusts into their topical dialogue.

The main feature of their verbal effectiveness became known as the "wisecrack"—a specific type of gag. The wisecrack destroys someone or something fast and mercilessly. It is a flippant oneliner, and from Kaufman's pen it usually sounded sardonic. The wisecrack is quickly introduced within the first few minutes of *Dulcy* when Bill Parker (Dulcy's brother) converses with Gordon Smith (Dulcy's husband) about the state of business:

> GORDON. I say, how's business?
> BILL. (*As though announcing a death*) Haven't you heard?
> GORDON. (*A bit cheerily*) Oh, I don't know—I have an idea it may be picking up presently.
> BILL. (*Tapping the newspaper*) You've been reading Mr. Schwab. (*He quotes*) "Steel Man Sees Era of Prosperity."
> GORDON. Well—I think he's right, at that.
> BILL. Yes. (*A pause*) Rockefeller expects to break even this year, too.

Bill's line about Rockefeller ushered in the era of the wisecrack. Later in the decade Kaufman and the wisecrack became synonymous.

Another Kaufmanian feature woven into this play is the inclusion of either remarks about or the actual playing of card games. *Dulcy* incorporates the start of a bridge game as act 1 concludes. Kaufman loved to play poker and bridge, and stories about his card-playing abilities and antics are legion. (He was eventually recognized as a bridge expert by Charles Goren, the leading bridge exponent.) The rituals involved in playing cards become one of Kaufman's theatrical motifs used either as a comic device, or for character revelation, or to set the mood of the scene.

Dulcy became the first Broadway success shared by Kaufman and Connelly. In the beginning of the 1920s, when one hundred consecutive performances were uncommon, *Dulcy* enjoyed a run of 246 performances. It was followed by a successful tour, then selected by Burns Mantle for his annual book, *The Best Plays of 1921–22.* Finally the script was purchased by Joseph M. Schenck, an independent film producer, and the script was the basis for three different films: 1923 with Constance Talmadge in the Fontanne role, 1930 with Marion Davies as Dulcy (retitled *Not So Dumb*), and 1940 with Ann Sothern.

Kaufman and Connelly did not rest on their newly acquired laurels, and producers and publishers were soon bidding for their talents. They accepted an offer from Arthur Samuels of *Life,* a humor magazine, to provide a monthly calendar that combined accurate historical data with whimsies they created. This activity covered December 1921 through November 1922.

The two writers also agreed to write another play for Tyler. This time he wanted a vehicle for Helen Hayes, whom Tyler had managed since 1917. Her successes while still a teenager were in James M. Barrie's *Dear Brutus* in 1918 and Booth Tarkington's *Clarence.* She was appearing in the title role of *Pollyanna* as it toured the country when Kaufman and Connelly began creating an adult role for her in *To the Ladies!*

The play was written to satirize big business. It was to be different from *Dulcy,* which approached business dealings from the executive level. The new script was to examine the rise of an ordinary white-collar employee. Modern business practices of the early 1920s are scrutinized in general, but each act focuses on a particular aspect of climbing the ladder of success: Creating the appropriate image; making a lasting impression; and succeeding after promotion.

In *To the Ladies!* newlyweds Leonard and Elsie Beebe plan how to advance Leonard's career at the piano manufacturing company where he works as a clerk. When the play commences, Leonard has succeeded in attracting the attention of the owner of the company, Mr. Kincaid, and act 1 centers on the impending Saturday afternoon visit of Mr. and

Mrs. Kincaid to the Beebes' Nutley, New Jersey, apartment. As a result of the visit, Leonard is invited to speak at the company's annual banquet, an honor that insures his eligibility for a promotion.

The banquet dominates act 2: Scene 1 shows the Beebes preparing to go to the event; scene 2 satirizes company banquets. For his presentation, Leonard has memorized a speech from the book "Five Hundred Speeches for All Occasions." His opponent for the chief-clerk position is asked by the toastmaster to speak first, and this young aspirer delivers exactly the same address Leonard planned to give. Elsie rescues her shaken husband by giving an impromptu talk for him since she claims he is suffering from laryngitis. Her speech, which lauds Mr. Kincaid's general acumen, is a resounding success, and Leonard is promoted.

Act 3 opens with Leonard ensconced in the outer office of Mr. Kincaid's suite serving as Kincaid's righthand man. Tom Baker, the defeated candidate, discovers that Leonard never created the speech Elsie gave for him and blurts out this information to Mr. Kincaid. Leonard is demoted, and Elsie once more saves the day for her ambitious, but dull husband. The famous line from this play occurs during Elsie's defense session with Mr. Kincaid: "Nearly all great men have been married, it can't be merely a coincidence." Mrs. Kincaid unexpectedly arrives in the office and assists Elsie in getting her husband reinstated to his former position. It becomes obvious that Mrs. Kincaid advises her husband on all major company decisions. Leonard is delighted to learn that he has regained his position on a permanent basis. The play underlines the notion that in business someone with imagination must help the industrious dullards to succeed.

To the Ladies! received excellent reviews, but it was less successful at the box office (128 performances) than *Dulcy*. The day after *To the Ladies!* opened at the Liberty Theatre on Broadway, the 21 February 1922, review in the *New York Times* called it "a wise and merry and artful comedy." Two paragraphs later the reviewer says that the play "leads up to a single scene which for caustic and quite devastating humor, has not often been approached by American playwrights." The scene is the company banquet, which was considered an American institution.

Arthur Hobson Quinn selected *To the Ladies* as one of five important plays produced from 1917 to 1922 to be included in his 1923 volume, *Contemporary American Plays*. Quinn believed that it was truly representative of a national drama that was beginning to receive recognition.

With the emergence of Eugene O'Neill who had nine plays produced between 1920 and 1922 including *The Emperor Jones, The Hairy Ape,* and *Anna Christie*—American theater could begin to boast of vigorous dramas of ideas. O'Neill's serious plays quickly began to command respect internationally as well as at home. American drama was in the hands of a few new dramatists who were creating modern dramas. Kaufman was included in this group of moderns: he did not write the genteel comedies of his predecessors; his art of spoofing was executed with vigor and ingenuity that had not been a part of the American stage. Quinn perceived the stature of O'Neill and Kaufman, and how they were contributing to his dream of a recognized national drama.

Quinn also believed that *To the Ladies!* was more significant than *Dulcy.* He claims that the theme, which appealed to the most dramatists in the season of 1921–22, is that of married life.[4] What makes *To the Ladies!* more significant than either *Dulcy* or its other competitors is that "the playwrights (Kaufman and Connelly) have seized upon the great fact that the most precious things in life are our illusions, especially those we begin to suspect ourselves, ..."[5]

To the Ladies! does have interesting and significant views about marriage, but it also comments most poignantly about life in America—especially for the youthful middle class who are struggling to achieve success. Elsie addresses the basic issue when she speaks on Leonard's behalf at the banquet: "It seems to me that about everybody in the world has written a book or designed a chart or advertised some kind of university course in the magazines that will show you how to get a personality by mail, make friendships according to science, or strengthen your character by mathematics. A great many people have apparently been trying to find human nature all laid out and classified in textbooks and on maps."

This play is timely in its issues even though some of the events are dated. Certainly the wisdom of Elsie and Mrs. Kincaid would appeal to contemporary feminists. The play may have struck too close to home on several levels to be enjoyed thoroughly when it was first produced; therefore, *Dulcy,* in which the main character posed no threat to anyone and whose arrows aimed at business did not send a quiver through the audience, had a longer run. *To the Ladies!* toured after it closed on Broadway, and it was filmed twice. The first film appearing in 1923 was produced by Famous Players-Lasky, which soon merged with Paramount Pictures. The second version was produced in 1934 by Paramount (and retitled *Elmer and Elsie*).

Despite the fact that *To the Ladies!* was not a smash hit, its revenues improved the standard of living for its creators. The Kaufmans moved to a more spacious apartment, and Connelly reportedly bought a riding habit, although he did not as yet own a horse.[6]

Revues

Nineteen twenty-two continued to be a productive year for Kaufman and Connelly, but they also managed to engage in special theatrical activities just for fun. The first project came soon after *To the Ladies!* opened, when the Vicious Circle decided to put on its own show, "No Sirree!" It would have one performance, on 30 April 1922, and admission would be by invitation only. All the parts were played by the Round Tablers, who also had written the sketches and lyrics of their show, which was a parody of a Russian revue "Chauve Souris" that was popular on Broadway that season. "No Sirree!" was billed as an Anonymous Entertainment by the Vicious Circle of the Hotel Algonquin. The opening chorus consisted of the authors of the revue: Alexander Woollcott, John Peter Toohey, Robert C. Benchley, George S. Kaufman, Marc Connelly, and Franklin P. Adams. They were attired in bathrobes and lyrically explained that they had written this show to suit themselves.[7]

Kaufman's major contribution for the revue was a sketch called "Big Casino is Little Casino," a parody of the explicit moral melodramas written by Samuel Shipman. Woollcott played the role of Dregs the butler, Kaufman was John Findlay—a young attorney and the romantic lead, Frank Adams was detective O'Brien, Connelly was a convict, and Robert E. Sherwood was governor of New York. The remaining roles were played by other members of the Round Table. Kaufman claims in his introduction to the script that "this play is designed to contain a little bit of each of the many things that have been keeping people away from the theatre in recent years." He further contends that "although its title might indicate that it is aimed at a particular playwright addicted to paradoxical titling, the play as a whole is intended to cover a much wider ground."[8]

The play begins in the home of Henry C. Archibald, a multimillionaire who is giving a lavish party for 214 rich guests. When John Findley, a rising young district attorney, arrives, he quickly gets into a heated debate with his host on the reason for criminality. Findley reminds Archibald about the daughter that the multimillionaire cast out when she opposed her father's views regarding criminals. The two men begin to play a game of cards when catastrophe strikes: The new deck has only fifty-one cards. An outraged Archibald immediately sits down to write a letter of protest to the American Playing Card Company.

Three days later a detective arrives with news that the missing card was the ten of diamonds, which means "Big Casino." The factory girl who packed the deck is outside, and she is on her way to the penitentiary as punishment for her misdeed. The culprit is Margaret, Archibald's cast-out daughter. She tells her father that his philosophy regarding "riches are everything" is bad. He represents Big Casino and she is Little Casino.

Two days later Archibald is with his broker and is sincerely trying to go into bankruptcy. A little old man keeps buying all the shares Archibald is selling. When Archibald loses all his money, the little old man reveals that "he" is Margaret in disguise. She restores all his stock to him for he has proven himself a good man. She proclaims him to be Big Casino, and Archibald admits that "Big Casino is Little Casino, after all."

The satire of the piece certainly highlights the weaknesses of many vacuous melodramas that were popular in the theater of the period. The play is very short but obviously packed with reversals, complication after complication, cast-out family members, stubborn parents, moral questions, and it drips with sentimentality. It is a good example of what a meaningful, modern script should not be.

Another Kaufman and Connelly contribution staged for "No Sirree!" was an autobiographical song sung by the authors. Seven years later Alexander Woollcott recalled that Kaufman was costumed in sombero, spurs, and chaps. These two tall performers—Kaufman was spare and thick-haired while Connelly was even taller, rounded, and balding— won approval both for their lyrics and for their rendition of them. Woollcott, claiming to recall the exact lyrics, reproduced them in his *New Yorker* article:

> Oh we are Kaufman and Connelly
>   from Pittsburgh,
> We're Kaufman and Connelly
>   from the West,
> It's true no one has asked me yet,
> But in New York it's etiquette,

To wear a 24-sheet on your
    chest.
So will the managers please give
    us their attention?
The Algonquin is where we can be
    addressed.
We have no wish to embarrass,
Samuel H. or William Harris,
But we're Kaufman and Con-
    nelly.
We're Kaufman and Connelly
We're Kaufman and Connelly
From the West.[9]

The spirit of these two men who had recently found success working together seems to emanate from the ditty. Their performance received the most praise from actress Laurette Taylor who stood in as the *New York Times* critic of the evening: "I think the two who will come out of it the best now will be the ones that would have no nonsense but came downstage and sang, 'I'm Kaufman and that's Connelly!'"

Obviously "No Sirree!" proclaimed exclusiveness and mutual admiration among the cast members, but it was created for a special audience. Kaufman and Connelly approached George Tyler with the proposal of producing a similar Broadway revue featuring the Round Tablers. They wanted it to be intimate in scale and thoroughly satirical, but they failed to realize, as did their fellow contributors, that they needed to create less esoteric materials. Tyler did produce "The 49ers," which opened on 7 November 1922.

Kaufman's contribution to this bagatelle is "Life in the Back Pages." This sketch presents a "typical" American middle-class family relaxing in their living room shortly before dinner. The situation reveals that the family and their visitors converse in the language of advertisements. These individuals are finding love, riches, and satisfaction from self-improvement literature. They are also industrious folks who are working the additional-income schemes they have learned about from magazines and newspaper ads. The play seems hastily conceived with themes previously satirized in a more clever manner by Kaufman.

"The 49ers" was not well received. Woollcott, who did not take a part in this revue, stated in his *New York Times* review that the evening had a "hit or miss showmanship about it." Also the humor was too inbred for the general public, and the material left the audience puzzled and not thoroughly entertained as a revue was expected to do. Tyler closed the revue two weeks after it had opened.

Ragging Hollywood

Kaufman and Connelly continued to work on full-length plays while dabbling with the two revues. They wrote *Merton of the Movies,* an adaptation of the novel by Harry Leon Wilson, and a comedy that toured the tryout circuit as "West of Pittsburgh." Malcolm Goldstein discusses how these two plays offered a comment on the cultural change that was taking place in small towns across America.[10] This was a time when residents from small towns began to be envious of the glamour of city life and its many amenities. They hoped either to capture some of those benefits at home or to seek them elsewhere.

Frank Adams introduced Kaufman and Connelly to the Wilson novel, which was being serialized in the *Saturday Evening Post.* This story about the silent-film era of Hollywood appealed to the two playwrights so they negotiated for the stage rights and granted Wilson half of the royalty. Tyler agreed to produce *Merton of the Movies*: it opened 13 November 1922.

Merton Gill, a young clerk at Gashwiler's General Store in Simsbury, Illinois, is obsessed with the dream to become a movie actor in serious films. He has prepared for his Hollywood career by saving money to move West, taking mail-order acting lessons, and engaging in other activities to secure film work. In act 2 Merton arrives in Hollywood to try his luck at the casting office of Holden Pictures, where Beulah Baxter, the "wonder woman of the silver screen," makes her adventure films. Merton's high ideals are the result of his gullibility and naiveté. He believes that the adventure films starring Baxter and her romantic co-hero, Harold Parmalee, are the finer artistic endeavors of the film industry. On the other hand, he disdains the comedies made by director Jeff Baird that star "the cross-eyed man." Slowly his illusions are destroyed on the studio lot of Holden Pictures. A shattered Merton is rescued by the Montague Girl, who works as an extra and a stunt woman at the studio. She gets Merton a starring role in a Baird comedy, but everyone conspires to trick him into thinking he is making a "serious" film.

Following the premier of his film, a destroyed Merton wanders the streets of Los Angeles because the audience laughed during his scenes.

Upon his return to his boardinghouse the next morning, Merton discovers that he is regarded as a brilliant new comic talent. His shame of having been tricked into starring in comedy quickly dissipates as he adjusts to success and acquires an altered perspective of his work.

This four-act, six-scene comedy won acclaim by the critics and proved to be the biggest Kaufman-and-Connelly box office success with a run of 398 performances. The play was selected by Burns Mantle for *The Best Plays of 1922–23*, and the film rights were sold. The plot became a popular vehicle concerned with the movie business and as a result it was filmed three times: 1924, 1932 (*Make Me a Star*), and 1947 starring Red Skelton.

Merton of the Movies was the first in a series of burlesques about Hollywood. Kaufman had the Broadway writers' skepticism about life and work in Hollywood even though he had not been there. He continually mocked films and movie people in his plays. The tradition started with "Third Man High," progressed in *Dulcy,* and was in high gear with *Merton of the Movies.* Later, Kaufman would devote another entire play to the general topic when he and Moss Hart wrote *Once in a Lifetime.*

For *Merton of the Movies* Kaufman and Connelly made more imaginative use of the stage than they did in their earlier plays. *Dulcy* requires a unit set, which was not unusual for plays of that era, and lends itself to less expensive production costs. With success came the ability to command a bigger production budget. Therefore, *To the Ladies!* requires three different sets; "Merton" requires six locations that creates the effect of mobility like that seen in films. Kaufman and Connelly worked to break the conventional dramatic mold of one or two sets often dictated by parsimonious producers. These two playwrights—like Eugene O'Neill whose *The Hairy Ape* opened the same season—attempted a more cinematographic approach to locale.

New technology, philosophy, and talents were also at work to change the history of stage design. Scene designers, led by Robert Edmond Jones and Lee Simonson, were translating the work of the newer playwrights into visually expressive theater. Kaufman and Connelly were in the vanguard of modernism in the American theater.

After "Merton" opened and before settling down to rewrite "The Deep Tangled Wildwood," Kaufman and Connelly wrote a short parody of Charles Dickens's *A Christmas Carol.* The script was published in the December 1922 issue of *The Bookman.* This tale recounts dour Scrooge's conversion to kindness as inspired by Tiny Tim saying "God bless us every one." Following this personality change, the Cratchet family and Scrooge go into the kindness business, which prospers. The Kindness Trust tries to take over the business, but clever Tiny Tim has anticipated the maneuver and succeeded in buying out the trust without its knowledge. This is another spoof on American business practices especially those related to putting Christmas on a business basis.

That Old Hometown

The play that toured in May 1922, but required revisions before opening on Broadway was "West of Pittsburgh." This script was renamed "Turn to the Left," then "Little Old Millersville," soon it became "The Old Home Town," and prior to its opening on 5 November 1923, it was retitled "The Deep Tangled Wildwood." Perhaps the constant changing of title hints that there were some problems with the script. Marc Connelly recalls that he and Kaufman "would seek the comment and advice of more experienced people and thus minimize the likelihood of error."[11] The play followed too many paths, lacked unity, and needed more character development.

Kaufman and Connelly believed that luck had a lot to do with their first two Broadway successes. This script was their third, and the basic idea for the play was very different from their earlier endeavors. Also their intention was to create "an ironic comedy about a tired, blasé New York playwright who goes back to the small town of his birth to recapture the simplicities of life his years in the city made him forget."[12] The fun was to evolve from his discovering that bucolic Millersville had changed to an urban center as sophisticated and corrupt as any metropolitan area. The playwrights also intended to spoof the "plays in which folksiness was commingled with a mildly melodramatic plot about financial skullduggery."[13]

During the prologue, playwright James Parks Leland reveals to his trusted friend, Harvey Wallick, a desire to return to his hometown of Millersville. Leland believes his talent has gone stale in New York City and living in Millersville would restore his creativity. In act 1 Jim arrives in Millersville to discover that a dye plant had moved to the town and changed the life-style of the community. Millersville is now a metropolis with a movie theater, two newspapers, a new radio station, a speedway, and most of the trappings of all big cities. The people have become citified, particularly in their activities and morals, and even Jim's Aunt Sarah and his old girlfriend Mary Ellen have developed affected manners. The only person who seems to have retained the important values of life cherished by Jim is Phyllis Westley. She returned to Millersville from New York where she studied to be an artist. Her uncle supported her studies even though he could not afford the expense (shades of "The Failure").

Harvey Wallick comes to visit Jim in act 2 and begins to assist Jim in his efforts to correct the errors of the people. Scene 2 is devoted to the opening of the new radio station. Jim, thinking that the microphone is turned off, tells the citizenry that they have turned their town into "a ten-cent make-believe metropolis." The speech was actually broadcast, and the results are revealed in act 3 when many people tell Jim the effects his speech had on each of them. Mary Ellen gives up Jim to marry a man being transferred to New York City. Jim is then free to propose to Phyllis, who accepts. They decide to live happily ever after in New York.

There seems to be a dichotomy in the thinking of the hero. He decides that he does not wish to give up the advantages of living in New York, but he expects the population of his hometown to return to the ruralism that existed prior to World War I. Also the hero is a sham who lacks the qualities that make Kaufman and Connelly's other protagonists endearing. Jim is not humorous like Dulcy, not wise like Elsie, nor really naive like Merton.

There are other weaknesses in the plotting of the script. Pieces of the plot are left unresolved—especially those related to property troubles besetting Phyllis's uncle. Once Kaufman and Connelly begin spoofing the specific advances made in Millersville, the plot and characters are sacrificed for the wit and satire. The New York critics were not receptive to the play, and it closed after its sixteenth performance.

Musicals

Early in 1923 Kaufman and Connelly were approached by Rufus LeMaire, a novice producer, to write the book (script) for a musical comedy. The team of Bert Kalmar (lyrics) and Harry Ruby (music) were already signed for this project. The book for this musical could be on any topic the playwright chose; however, the material would have to fit a preselected title: "Helen of Troy, New York." "Neither George nor I thought the title very clever, but it did suggest a narrative that we thought could be funny," said Marc Connelly.[14]

The plot revolves around the executives and employees of the Yarrow Collar Factory in Troy, New York—the collar capital of the world.

Helen works in the Efficiency Department; she is efficient, her boss is not. She is fired by her jealous supervisor, but not before David Williams—the son of a former partner in Yarrow—falls in love with her. There is much ado about an advertising campaign to promote a new collar, an encouraged love interest between David and Grace (daughter of Mr. Yarrow), a celebration of the fiftieth anniversary of the company, and other plot complications—several of which are triggered by Helen's outspoken kid sister Maribelle.

The scene shifts in act 2 to New York City. It is several weeks after the events in Troy. Maribelle is working as a model, and Helen is searching for a job without any success. Mr. Yarrow and his factory entourage converge on the photographic studio where Maribelle is working, and "the wooden horse" is brought forth. Mr. Yarrow attempts to get out of his three-year contract with the head of the Efficiency Department. His ruse is to act in an irrational manner by selling his factory to the male collar model for a five-hundred-dollar option and a total price of five thousand dollars. Unbeknownst to Yarrow, David makes the deal viable by establishing a bank account to cover the option payment. His father, in a moment of desperation, follows Yarrow's example and makes the same deal with the male model, using his shares of the business. Yarrow and Williams learn that the options are real and will be exercised by David, Helen, Maribelle, and the male model, whom Grace loves. Helen tricks the devious head of the Efficiency Department with her own "wooden horse"; she wins the new collar design award. Success seems assured for the new partnership, and marriages are planned by Helen and David as well as by Grace and the male model.

The plot rambles, the book is wordy, the romances lack embraces and sparks, but even so, the satire on business was enjoyed by the New York audiences. The production had a run of 193 performances. It is always difficult to judge a musical without its music, dance, and spectacle. This production was obviously successful, and its successors would include *The Pajama Game* and *How to Succeed in Business without Really Trying*.

The offer to write a second musical book came in the early fall of 1924. Producers Sidney Wilmer and Walter Vincent made the proposal to Kaufman and Connelly after having signed Lewis Gensler and Milton Schwarzwald to write the score with additional lyrics by Ira Gershwin. Though Gershwin had contributed lyrics to other Broadway shows, he had previously used the pseudonym Arthur Francis, for he wanted to gain a reputation on his own before using the family name that was associated with his successful brother, composer George Gershwin. "Be Yourself" marks the first credit Ira Gershwin would receive under the family name.

Kaufman and Connelly had written a musical script titled "Miss Moonshine" during their early years of collaboration, which they believed suitable for Wilmer and Vincent's production. This script was revamped a bit, set to music, and retitled "Be Yourself." The plot is set in Tennessee, where the mountaineers mingle freely with the visitors from New York.[15] A plot summary can not be accurately recounted since there is no known extant copy of this play. The manuscript was never submitted for copyright, which is most unusual for Kaufman, whose pattern was to obtain a copyright for all plays he wrote.

The show opened on 23 September 1924, at the Sam H. Harris Theatre. Reviewers may have been a bit blasé that evening since the record-breaking operetta *Rose Marie* had opened the previous night. However, "Be Yourself" was reviewed in the *New York Times* as having "the funniest first act that has been played in these parts for many years." The reviewer went on to say that the rest of the script is pretty much average musical-comedy fare. The production ran for ninety-three performances.

Prelude to Parting

Winthrop Ames, one of Broadway's prestigious producers with a reputation for good taste and great imagination, wanted Kaufman and Connelly to adapt the German expressionistic *Hans Sonnenstössers Höllenfahrt* play by Paul Apel. Connelly recalls the meeting with Ames when they told him the original play's fresh technique was more interesting than the plot.[16] Ames was delighted, for he wanted the playwrights to create an American story using Apel's method of dreamlike association.

Ames gave the playwrights only a plot outline—not a translation of the entire script. Since Kaufman and Connelly were neither tied philosophically nor stylistically to the waning movement of Expressionism, they used expressionistic features indiscriminately. Within a few days they constructed a rough outline of the story, the basic theme being the ancient conflict between art and materialism.[17] The team took a minor product of the German expressionistic movement and completely rewrote it within an American setting.

Expressionism attempts to address the basic reality of its subjects rather than to reproduce the mere appearance of reality; therefore, the representation of reality is distorted to communicate an inner vision. The revelation of emotional aspects of the subject was one of the desired expressionistic effects that is especially evident in the drama. The movement was a revolt against the art and the civilization that existed during the first two decades of this century. The condition of human society, of which the arts are a stage of development, was considered to be superficially prosperous and attractive, but rotten to the core. Some distinguishing features of German Expressionism include distortions or exaggerations of specific aspects of the environment, displays of sharp breaks with reality, labels for characters rather than names, outbursts of exclamatory and dynamic dialogue, and lessons on social concerns.

When Kaufman and Connelly wrote their script titled *Beggar on Horseback,* they created two styles of action within the work: realistic and dream. The realistic scenes take place in the apartment of the protagonist, Neil McRae; the dream sequence uses elements of the expressionistic style. The playwrights incorporated a pantomime suggested by Ames that includes music and movement even though nonmusical plays did not usually include a segment with music. As a result there is no one specific style in the production. Therefore, John Corbin of the *New York Times* describes the play as a parody of Expressionism, which seems like an accurate assessment of the work.[18]

Neil McRae, a talented composer of serious music, struggles to survive while maintaining a commitment to his art. His only piano student is a young woman named Gladys Cady, who is a member of a wealthy family that used to live in Neil's hometown. Dr. Albert Rice, a boyhood friend of Neil's, urges the composer to take advantage of Gladys's apparent romantic interest and to marry her for financial security. In a state of overexhaustion, Neil takes the sleeping pills given to him by Albert.

During this sleep Neil dreams of his life as it would be if he were to marry Gladys. He also dreams of his love for Cynthia Mason, his neighbor across the hall. Neil's dream turns violent and he is suddenly in a courtroom where he is on trial for murdering the Cady family. His motive for the murder was the need to write his music. The jury finds Neil guilty of murder and of creating highbrow music. He is sentenced to write songs at the Cady Art Factory.

Neil awakens from this nightmare to discover that Cynthia has changed her mind and no longer believes Neil should follow Albert's marriage advice. Neil extricates himself from his obligations to Gladys; he is free to write his music and to plan his life with Cynthia.

Beggar on Horseback was the most successful artistic product of the Kaufman and Connelly collaborations. It was both a critical and a box office success with a run of 224 performances. The critical acclaim heaped upon the play and its authors makes it a benchmark in the annals of American dramatic literature. From its 1924 opening-night reviews until 1964, when Joseph Mersand included it in his book, *Three Plays about Business in America,* the play continued to win praise.

The reviewer for the *New York Times* comments in his 13 February 1924 review that the audience grew more delighted with the play since "it bristles with sly and caustic satire, brims with novel and richly colored theatric inventions, and overflows with inconsequent humor and motley spirit of youth." Midway in the review, the range of topics tackled by the playwrights is described as "art and letters, politics, crime and the newspapers, touching everything as it passes with the witches' fire of fancy and the dart of deadly satire." The enthusiastic commentator concludes his review: "The novelty alone of *Beggar on Horseback* would assure it an eager hearing, and it has the further advantage of being intelligently witty and inspired throughout by the richest and most varied good taste."

Another source of recognition that was declared newsworthy were comments made by noted British playwright John Galsworthy during his 1924 visit to the United States. Galsworthy mentioned only two plays when asked his opinions on American drama: *Anna Christie* and *Beggar on Horseback.* He believed that *Beggar on Horseback* was one of the most typically American things he had ever seen. "It was a fine satire on the America of the times."[19]

Critics Barrett Clark and George Freedley praise the play in their 1947 *A History of Modern Drama* as "the first genuinely imaginative satire of its kind that, without heat or apparent moral indignation, attempted to expose the barren machine-age efficiency that had to some extent become a religion to Homo Americanus."[20] While the theater had used big business as a subject in the early 1920s, the drama had not questioned the sacred aims and procedures of the business barons.

Professor Mersand, another of the theater historians and critics who perpetuated the play's reputation, points out that the basic truths expressed in the play were still very much in evidence in 1964.[21] In our space-age society we cannot escape the fact that those same truths are still viable. *Beggar on Horseback,* though rarely produced today, is an exciting theatrical work that easily lends itself to the technical innovations and staging techniques used in contemporary theater.

According to the 1976 *Ottemiller's Index to Plays in Collections, Beggar on Horseback* has been reprinted ten times in various anthologies as an example of American Expressionism. It was successfully produced in England during the 1924–25 season, and the Famous Players-Lasky made the 1925 film with Edward Everett Horton starring as Neil McRae. The play's popularity in New York also warranted a request for Kaufman and Connelly to write a brief parody of it for the revue "Round the Town."

Revues are popular entertainments that had their Golden Age in America between 1915 and 1930. They survey contemporary events with songs, topical sketches (short plays), dances, burlesques, and monologues. The type of revue in which Kaufman participated tended to be the intimate revues relying more on wit and satire than on spectacular costumes, dancing, and dozens of beautiful show girls, which were of the Zeigfeld Follies tradition.

"Round the Town," which opened 21 May 1924, featured "Beggar Off Horseback" as a sketch. In this parody, Neil is a rotten musician whose ambition is to marry Gladys, the rich girl, and to become a successful, wealthy, ticket speculator. During the dream sequence Neil learns what married life would be like at the poverty level with the lovely but poor Cynthia as his bride. When he awakens, he discovers Gladys is present because she needs to marry him; she is pregnant. He decides to marry her and her family's money. The revue's survival rate was fourteen performances: "Beggar Off Horseback" was then assigned to the repository for most topical material—oblivion.

Parting

The question raised in 1924, after "Be Yourself," is why did this successful playwriting duo separate? Connelly's autobiographical account in *Voices Offstage* merely states their last major collaboration was "Be Yourself." He elaborates by confirming that "our personal friendship continued until his death, however, and privately neither of us hesitated to call on the other for advice and help."[22]

Kaufman was a writer driven to be productive. It is amazing to consider that he maintained a full-time job as a newspaper drama editor while he also wrote Broadway plays and revue sketches. Throughout his career, Kaufman looked beyond the project at hand to several future endeavors; frequently he worked on two scripts simultaneously. It seems likely that Connelly, with his acquired success and financial gains, did not wish to maintain the pace set by Kaufman. This idea is corroborated by a comment Kaufman made to Howard Teichmann many years later. Kaufman mentioned that Connelly was constantly late for work, and often missed entire sessions. Kaufman grew tired of Connelly's excuses and finally said, "Marc, someday New York harbor will freeze over and you'll write the best damn play anyone's ever seen."[23] (Part of the prophecy came true, Connelly wrote *The Green Pastures,* which won the Pulitzer Prize for drama in 1930.) Thus, the partnership just dissolved without any formal announcements. Suddenly it became evident that the 1925–26 Broadway theater season would not have a new Kaufman and Connelly play.

Afterward

Kaufman and Connelly teamed up again for the 1932 show of the Dutch Treat Club—a theatrical club that Kaufman joined in the mid–1920s. This show included a sketch titled "Service" written and performed by the two western Pennsylvanians. This playlet, written during the Great Depression, reveals the frustration of selling theater tickets. Kaufman played a ticket broker confronted by Connelly, a most demanding customer who desires a ticket to a play but who wishes not to pay for it. The customer says that the play he wants to see should be similar to George Kelly's *The Show Off* (1924) and Jerome Kern's *Sally* (1920). The cast should feature half a dozen stars such as Ed Wynn, Alfred Lunt, the Marx Brothers, and maybe the Warner Brothers, who he heard were good, too. The beleaguered broker suggests sending these stars to the customer's home for the performance, and the customer believes the idea is acceptable—as long as ushers are part of the free deal.

The piece comments once again on theater ticket vendors; however, the customer is the target of the satire. Undoubtedly it appealed to an audience composed of theater people, and its success may have inspired Kaufman and Connelly to create another sketch for the 1933 Dutch

Treat Club show. Malcolm Goldstein reports that they wrote and performed in "Or What Have You?"[24] Several decades later Kaufman and Connelly began working on a satirical musical play about the extravagant adventures of a Jimmy-Hoffa-type labor leader.[25] This work commenced a few weeks before Kaufman died in 1961.

Chapter Three
Other Options
Solo

Prior to the demise of the Kaufman/Connelly partnership, Kaufman, undoubtedly, considered the option that would allow his continued productivity as a playwright. His obvious alternative was to write by himself. He had done that, somewhat successfully, before he met Connelly, and he had continued to write a few revue sketches alone during their years of collaboration. One sketch in particular must have given him even more confidence to try solo writing. *If Men Play Cards as Women Do* opened on 22 September 1923 in Irving Berlin's *Third Music Box Revue*. For at least three decades it was one of the most popular one-act plays in the United States.

The idea for the sketch came most unexpectedly on an afternoon when Kaufman decided to visit his mother and discovered that she was having a card party. As he listened to the conversation, he was struck by the lack of attention the ladies gave to the cards, and drawn to their devotion to verbal exchanges of stories and tidbits. He thought this situation could be even more amusing if the characters were four men playing poker, but conducting themselves in the chatty manner he had witnessed.[1] Supposedly he sat down that evening and wrote the play, which is a gem of a one-act, with a style that is typical Kaufman: witty, tight, and terse.

For the 1925–26 season Kaufman wrote *The Butter and Egg Man*. It opened 23 September 1925, and it was a box office success with a run of 241 performances. The title was taken from a phrase familiar to New Yorkers who used it to refer to any naive out-of-towner with money. Joe Lehman and Jack McClure ("Mac") are searching for a butter and egg man to finance their latest theatrical production. Mac finds twenty-one-year-old Peter Jones from Chillicothe, Ohio, who buys into the production that has a disastrous opening in Syracuse. During an after-the-opening conference Joe fires his secretary Jane for intervening in the discussion. Peter, who adores Jane, becomes angry and puts up an option to buy the entire production from Joe and Mac. Peter now seeks a butter and egg man and lands Oscar Fritchie, the theatre-struck assistant manager of the hotel, where they all are staying.

Peter and Oscar rework the script and open the play on Broadway, where it is an instant success. Immediately an attorney-at-law representing an unknown writer claims the script was adapted from his client's short story. For this act of plagiarism he demands two-thirds of all profits. While Peter holds the attorney at bay, Joe decides to buy back the show since he hears the police may try to close it because the play features a brothel scene. The prospect of free publicity also convinces Mac to buy back the production. Peter arranges for both former producers to join forces, and he sells the problem-ridden production to them for one hundred thousand dollars. Peter plans to return with Jane and Oscar to Chillicothe and to go into the hotel business.

Once again the review in the *New York Times* (24 September 1925) addresses the basic issues. "The amusement that Mr. Kaufman's play affords comes as much from the dialogue as from invention." Within the same paragraph, an elaboration of this statement mentions that "the patter is bright, abounding in 'wisecracks,' and the lines are highly charged with sardonic, ill-mannered humor. The structure of the play is quite as full of surprise and entertainment."

Kaufman used the plot reversals he practiced during his apprenticeship years, but perfected with Connelly. He also employed other features that helped to make the Kaufman/Connelly collaborations successful. The naive, polite, young protagonist Peter is similar to Merton Gill, and the small-town backgrounds of both of these youngsters do not prepare them for the more sophisticated way of life found in the New York or Hollywood entertainment industries. Kaufman, however, allows Peter to become savvy. He is able to steer a failing situation onto a successful course and eventually outsmart his former partners. Also Peter receives assistance in his efforts—as does Merton—from a knowledgeable ingenue who protects and promotes him.

Other details, in the comedy pattern à la Kaufman and Connelly, used in *The Butter and Egg Man* include the secondary woman who is knowing and witty: Fanny, Joe Lehman's wife, fills the role in this play. And, too, the opening-night conference is a gathering of people with a common interest and need to indulge in praise or commiseration. It is similar in many ways to the company banquet in *To the Ladies!* and the pseudo town meeting staged at the radio station in

"The Deep Tangled Wildwood." In all three plays these second-act situations also share a moment of crisis for the protagonist who manages, usually through the assistance of another person, to overcome his problem and to move forward toward the stated goal.

Kaufman incorporated personal touches in *The Butter and Egg Man*. The events surrounding the short-story author's cry of plagiarism were undoubtedly inspired by a legal suit against Kaufman and Connelly on the same charge for "Helen of Troy, New York." (The charges were answered; Kaufman and Connelly were vindicated.)[2] Goldstein mentions another inside reference, which is the use of Chillicothe, Ohio, as Peter's hometown: this town was the birthplace of George C. Tyler, Kaufman's first producer.[3] Another device used by Kaufman is the inclusion of persons' proper names and titles of plays that would be recognizable to his audiences. Though this topical material may not be meaningful to contemporary audiences, it is one of the elements of Kaufman's work that underscores his status as a social historian.

Also of note, *The Butter and Egg Man* is Kaufman's first full-length play about Broadway theater and its people. Every one of his plays on this general subject displays a different facet of it. *The Royal Family* (1927, with Edna Ferber) is a portrait of a prominent family of actors; *Merrily We Roll Along* (1934, with Moss Hart) focuses on a playwright who chooses between art and commercial success; *Stage Door* (1936, with Ferber) illustrates the life of struggling young actresses; *The Fabulous Invalid* (1938, with Hart) is the history of a New York theater building; and *Bravo* (1948, with Ferber) shows a once-successful European playwright and other immigrant theater people trying to establish themselves in the United States after World War II.

Crosby Gaige, the producer of *The Butter and Egg Man,* tried to convince Kaufman to direct this play. The playwright conducted a few rehearsals, but reportedly lacked the self-confidence to direct his script.[4] It would be a few years before Kaufman's very successful debut as a director.

The Butter and Egg Man toured this country and in 1927 opened a successful run in London. It was translated into French, and was thus the first Kaufman script to be translated into another language. *Le Gentleman de l'Ohio* was published in the April 1927 issue of *Petite Illustration*. And following the sale of film rights, the script became the basis for five films: 1928, *The Butter and Egg Man* made by First National, a motion picture company formed in 1917, and eventually absorbed by Warner Brothers; 1932, *The Tenderfoot,* First National; 1937,

Dance Charlie, Dance made by Warners; 1940, *An Angel from Texas* released by Warners; and 1954, *Three Sailors and a Girl* remade by Warners.

Kaufman had his second opening of the season on 8 December 1925. The script was a musical entitled *The Cocoanuts,* with a score by Irving Berlin, and starring the Marx Brothers—Groucho, Chico, Harpo, and Zeppo. The idea for the Marx Brothers to play in a scripted musical comedy with book by George S. Kaufman came from Sam H. Harris, an established producer and ex-partner of George M. Cohan. Harris, who reputedly had a grasp of show business that was intuitive, thought Kaufman was capable of creating a script for the brothers incorporating their established comic styles and characterizations. This meant mingling the conventions of traditional comedic dramatic form with the Marx Brothers' impolite, unromantic, antisituation farce antics.

When offered this unusual opportunity, Kaufman, who was a friend of Harpo Marx, reportedly exclaimed, "I'd rather write for the Barbary apes."[5] The Marx Brothers' behavior on stage was unpredictable. They were known to indiscriminately add gags, make puns on lines, or incorporate chases whenever the mood struck any one of them to go for additional laughs. Kaufman, like most playwrights, did not fancy having his lines changed or cut by the performers. Yet he undertook the impossible and within several months created a satire based on the Florida land boom of 1925. Many stories have been recounted about the antics of the brothers and Kaufman's reactions throughout the rehearsal and performance period. The classic story occurred during the run of the play when Kaufman and Heywood Broun were standing backstage, watching the performance and chatting. Suddenly Kaufman interrupted Broun, who was talking, and walked closer to the stage. He returned to his irritated companion and explained, "I thought I heard one of the original lines of the show."[6]

The Cocoanuts is set in an undeveloped area of Florida. Henry W. Schlemmer, Groucho's character, owns and manages The Cocoanuts, a hotel and the surrounding lands located on Cocoanut Beach. Schlemmer stays busy throughout the play as he tries to make deals on his property. Two of the brothers—Harpo and Chico—are guests at the hotel, and their characters embrace the attributes that are usually associated with each of them. Harpo as Silent Sam—the mute clown dressed in battered hat, coat with trick sleeves, and coiffed with curls—played the harp at the appropriate time while Chico with his Italian dialect took his turn at rendering an unorthodox style of piano playing. For Zeppo, who lacked specific characteristics, Kaufman created the relatively small role of Jamison the hotel desk clerk.

This musical, like all others, has a love interest. Pretty Polly Potter, daughter of a wealthy matron, is romanced by aspiring architect Bob Adams, who is currently working as a clerk in the hotel. Their match is complicated by Bob's lack of wealth and position as well as by Mrs. Potter's preference for Harvey Yates to be her future son-in-law. Harvey, a young man of few scruples, joins a robbery scheme to relieve Mrs. Potter of her necklace evaluated at one hundred thousand dollars. The hiding place for the stolen gems is a tree stump on land that is being auctioned. Bob manages to buy that very piece of land just before the necklace is discovered in the stump. As a result of the jewel find, Bob is framed for the robbery and arrested. Mrs. Potter immediately announces that Polly will marry Harvey Yates. Bail is posted for Bob, who figures a way to trick Yates into revealing his connection with the robbery. The plan is successful: Bob is reunited with Polly; the land at Cocoanut Manor is sold due to Bob's architectural skills; and Groucho expresses interest in marrying Mrs. Potter.

The music by Irving Berlin was reviewed in the *New York Times* (9 December 1925) as "always pleasing," but *The Cocoanuts* did not have a single song that would become a Berlin classic. Supposedly Kaufman rejected a romantic ballad Berlin titled "Always."[7] Berlin believed Kaufman hated music and recalls that the playwright walked out of the theater whenever the music began.[8]

Despite the lack of a hit song, *The Cocoanuts* had a very successful production run of 375 performances on Broadway. The Marx Brothers took the show on tour for two years, made the film version in 1929, and became stars with this play as a vehicle. They loved the play and George S. Kaufman.[9]

Before the decade ended, Kaufman had also written two revue sketches for the Dutch Treat Club and the unsuccessful book for the musical "Strike Up the Band." The Dutch Treat offerings are *The Still Alarm* (1925) and "Shop Talk" (1926).

The Still Alarm is a spoof on the coolness of characters in English drawing-room comedies: politeness is key throughout the play. Two perfect gentlemen who are studying house plans in a hotel room are informed by a courteous bellboy that the hotel is on fire. There is no display of fear or haste in the entire situation. Two firemen arrive when the floor grows hot and smoke comes in the windows. The gentlemen show their good breeding by sitting down courteously to listen to one fireman play his violin. His partner explains that the musical fireman does not get much chance to practice at home, and the fireman hopes the gentlemen are "not anti-symphonic." The fire rages as they listen to a rendition of "Keep the Home Fires Burning."

This sketch was later the hit in a 1929 revue titled "The Little Show." The revue had a run of 321 Broadway performances. Samuel French published the play, and it remained a popular one-act for more than thirty years.

"Shop Talk" is set "any place where two men meet—a street, a corridor, anywhere." The characters, two undertakers in town for a professional convention, discuss business practices and conditions. This sketch is witty but, unlike *The Still Alarm,* "Shop Talk" lacks a definite style, a strong sense of situation, and character development.

Ferber

Prior to trying his act as a solo playwright, Kaufman—while still collaborating with Connelly in 1923—wrote to novelist Edna Ferber telling her that he had read her short story "Old Man Minick" and thought there was a play in it. Even though Ferber believed that audiences would not be interested in a play about an old man who goes to live with his son and daughter-in-law,[10] she did work with Kaufman on the adaptation.

At the time Kaufman and Ferber embarked on their playwriting project, her recently finished novel *So Big* was published. It became the winner of the 1924 Pulitzer Prize for fiction. Ferber was also experienced at adapting her McChesney stories into theater pieces. *Our Mrs. McChesney,* adapted by Ferber with a collaborator, was staged in 1915 and had a respectable run of 151 performances.

Both Ferber and Kaufman were equally well known for their achievements. For their first collaboration Kaufman established the policy that a collaborator's name would take precedence in the credits over his, when the partner was the initiator of the plot. If the collaborator created a novel or short story from which an adaption was made—or presented either a completed draft of the play, or outline, or idea—Kaufman could decide to place the partner's name before his.[11] For the first Kaufman/Ferber endeavor, Ferber's name was to precede Kaufman's.

Despite Kaufman's formula and the order of "Ferber and Kaufman" in the advertisements and programs, publisher Samuel French ignored this by designating "MINICK, A Comedy in Three Acts by George S. Kaufman and Edna Ferber" in the published version of the script. For this and other instances, Ferber was justified to lament that she was treated as a lesser light than Kaufman.

Minick opened on Broadway 24 September 1924, three weeks after "Be Yourself." Its run of 154 performances meant it bested that of the Kaufman/Connelly musical. The plot, while a bit thin, is touching. Fred and Nettie Minick prepare their Chicago apartment so that Fred's seventy-one-year-old father from Bloomington, Illinois, will be comfortable living with them. It is evident before the senior Minick's arrival that he will change the life-style of the young couple.

In act 2, within six months of his arrival, his habits cause the maid to quit, his daughter-in-law to become irritable, and his son to embark secretly on a new business venture. Minick's two aged companions, whom he met at the local park, urge him to move to a home for the elderly where they live. He immediately rejects the idea. Then he overhears a conversation of his daughter-in-law's that makes him reconsider his options, so when his friends tell him there is a vacancy in the home, he decides to move for the good of himself, his children's happiness, and his dream for grandchildren.

Stark Young's review in the *New York Times* (25 September 1924) comments that the story itself did not supply quite enough to last out three acts. He believes the play is "constantly funny, loving and tragic altogether." Ferber added more dimension to the characters than what was generally developed in the Kaufman/Connelly plays. Also *Minick* creates more emotional responses than earlier Kaufman endeavors. Ferber brought to her collaboration with Kaufman a touch of sentimentality that he could abide.

Kaufman disliked working with sentimental characters and story parts. Marc Connelly recalls that, "George would shiver slightly at my suggestion that he write at least a first draft of sentimental passages."[12] Sentimentality was a popular element in the drama because it was used in various ways to grip the emotions of the audience. Kaufman's aversion to sentimentality was based on its extravagant emotionalism, its extensive utilization by many playwrights, and its predictability.

Minick toured several of the major cities after it closed in New York and was a moderate success. It also had a good run in London, where it was revised to suit British tastes. Film rights were sold to Famous Players-Lasky, and the story was made and remade into films three times: 1925, titled *Welcome Home*; 1932, as *The Expert* by Warners; and

1939, *No Place to Go*. Even in the 1980s the story and characters probably could provide the seeds for a television situation comedy.

Ferber had a dividend from *Minick* that is beyond the rewards of financial gains and a successful play on Broadway. Following the tryout performance at the production conference, producer Ames tried to add some levity to the gathering and said: "Next time, we won't bother with tryouts. We'll all charter a showboat and we'll just drift down the rivers, playing the towns as we come to them, and we'll never get off the boat."[13] Ferber had never heard of a showboat, and after Ames explained what it was, she became excited about learning more about this interesting part of Americana. This, of course, was the moment that eventually led to her monumental novel, *Show Boat* (1926), and the musical of the same name that it inspired.

Kaufman and Ferber would write five more plays together over a twenty-four-year period (1925–48), for she was one collaborator he could return to nearly anytime he desired. From their collaborations came two major box office hits: *The Royal Family* (1927) and *Dinner at Eight* (1932).

The Royal Family was created by Kaufman and Ferber at the same time that Jerome Kern and Oscar Hammerstein were turning her novel *Show Boat* into a stunning musical. For eight months (November 1926 to June 1927) Kaufman and Ferber worked every morning beginning at eleven o'clock when Kaufman arrived at her apartment. Ferber describes her collaborator, upon his arrival at her door, as shaved, brushed, pressed, shined, wearing (among other things) one of his inexhaustible collection of quiet, rich ties.[14]

She reports that he was restless during their work sessions: he wanders about the room, ties and unties his shoestrings, does a few eccentric dance steps, and snoops about the room. She continues her inventory of his habits with "he eats prodigious quantities of chocolate candy and pastry"; he does not smoke or drink; he talks little; he rarely praises; he possesses a wit that is devastating but rarely cruel; and he is one of the most considerate of men.[15]

Their work on *The Royal Family* went well, but Kaufman divided his time between this project and "Strike Up the Band." The idea of writing a play about the private life of a family of actors was Ferber's. She was known for her sentimental portraits of American dynastic families, and this play is such a depiction.

The play is set in the familial home of the Cavendish family; its members represent three generations of actors. When the play begins, Fanny, the mother, a legendary actress is in her seventy-second year. Her two children are box office sensations: Julia is a Broadway star; and flamboyant, swashbuckling Tony has allowed Hollywood to lure him from the stage. Julia's daughter, Gwen, is a promising Broadway ingenue. Fanny's brother and his wife are a squabbling pair of thespians who try to outdo each other with aggrandized memories of past Broadway roles.

During the course of *The Royal Family* Julia decides to retire from the theater in order to marry an old flame from her youth and to move to South America. Gwen renounces the stage, marries, and produces a baby. Tony rushes home from Hollywood incognito while attempting to escape the clutches of an ardent female admirer. His stay is fleeting since the admirer is in hot pursuit; he dashes off to Europe. Fanny, who has been away from the stage for a couple of years because of poor health, begins to plan her next tour.

All of these plans are altered, in one way or another, in act 3, which takes place one year after acts 1 and 2. The play draws toward its final curtain as the family goes into the library to celebrate each one's decision to remain wedded to life on the stage. Fanny sits alone—happily savoring her joy that the entire family will soon be appearing in American theaters. Suddenly her drinking glass drops from her hand, her hand drops to her side; she is dead. The scene is held briefly as Julia comes into the room to find her mother.

It is a powerful ending to the play and different from anything else Kaufman had written prior to this play. Supposedly it was the ending he preferred to whatever else the collaborators may have developed.[16] It is not only emotionally charged, but it produces a stunning theatrical moment. At this time, Kaufman's awareness of using special moments for theatrical effect and impact was becoming highly developed.

The *New York Times* review (29 December 1927) records the rumor that "although the authors earnestly and officially disclaim specific models for their character portraits, the lobby scandal-mongers will chatter excitedly of the Barrymores." This family of American actors had been performing in the United States for three generations—Maurice and Georgie Drew Barrymore parented Ethel, John, and Lionel, who were the generation of the family active in theater in the 1920s. Ferber knew Ethel Barrymore, who starred in *Our Mrs. McChesney,* but Ferber avowed that the actress and her family did not inspire the Cavendish clan. There was one exception: the authors admitted that John Barrymore provided the model for handsome Tony, who deserted Broadway for Hollywood.

Whether the speculation about the Barrymores brought audiences to the theater or not hardly mattered since the play itself is excellent. Malcolm Goldstein's assessment of *The Royal Family* made fifty-two years after it opened is succinct: "The play has greater depth of characterization and considerably more humanity than any of Kaufman's earlier plays had. The combination of the two writers' skills was in balance throughout the writing, resulting in a work that is neither too sentimental nor too cynical. It has warmth, and it also has humor."[17]

The initial production produced by Jed Harris—no relation to Sam H. Harris, and Broadway's newest as well as most magnetic producer—ran for 343 performances, and was followed by a road tour. Film rights were sold to Paramount Pictures, who released the film in 1930 as *The Royal Family of Broadway.*

The *New York Times* review has a prophetic statement: "Mr. Kaufman and Miss Ferber have written a more resilient play than the performance expresses." This play was successfully revived in 1975 by Ellis Rabb for the American Bicentennial Theatre Production at the Mc-Carter Theatre in Princeton, New Jersey. It opened in New York on 30 December 1975, after limited engagements at the Kennedy Center in Washington, D.C., and at the Brooklyn Academy of Music. It has once again become a popular play enjoyed by audiences in this country and abroad.

Other Beginnings

The mid-1920s marked a continual period of transition for George S. Kaufman. His quest for new collaborators broadened; his family increased in 1925 with the addition of an adopted daughter named Anne; his career as a playwright experienced a few setbacks; his Algonquin friends continued to congregate at the hotel as well as expand their social activities; and his position as drama editor caused him to guard his professional integrity and avoid conflict-of-interest condemnation.

Corey Ford, one of the younger members of the Algonquin Wits, describes Kaufman during this period of his career: "Kaufman was always alone in the crowd, tall and gaunt, his hair brushed up high in a pompadour, a pair of tortoise-shell glasses riding well down on his nose, his eyes fixed on some invisible object on the ceiling. His fierce predatory look made headwaiters and taxi drivers quail; though actually he was painfully shy."[18]

It was sometime between 1923 and 1924 that Kaufman wrote a one-act play, "Wayward Bound," with Isabel Leighton. The surviving manuscript in the Library of Congress has a copyright date of 1924. Leighton did not appear to be either a regular or passing member of the Algonquin clan. She is Kaufman's only collaborator of the 1920s who does not seem to have any affiliation with the Vicious Circle; however, Leighton did have theatrical credentials as an actress. After this work with Kaufman, she eventually collaborated on at least five more plays with other playwrights, served as an associate editor of *Vogue* magazine, was a radio commentator, was an accredited war correspondent during World War II, and wrote several books.

"Wayward Bound" is a satire on a new set of dating problems confronting young women in the age of the automobile. The scene is a country road at night. A young woman, who has fled from her amorous date's clutches, discovers the benefits of joining the Society for the Assistance of Homewayward Girls. This organization was founded for the purpose of aiding females stranded in the country after they innocently accepted offers to go for automobile rides. The society provides transportation back home from the country: a pair of roller skates is given to each stranded female at rest-and-rescue stations established at two-mile intervals. The homeward-bound female is to check in at these stations as she progresses back toward the city. The young woman about to be indoctrinated into the society decides to accept a ride from a passing male instead of membership and security.

The vignette, which reads like a revue sketch, provides a delightful glimpse into a new social situation. The play displays the topical facet of Kaufman's wit, and illustrates how he taps into the tempo of the era.

In 1925 Herman J. Mankiewicz, Kaufman's assistant in the drama department at the *New York Times* and a fellow Algonquin Wit, wrote a revue sketch with Kaufman titled "Nothing Coming In." The setting is a pawnshop where two partners squabble over every transaction. Each customer creates a new dilemma for the partners, but the major conflict arises over the purchase of a fur coat for six dollars. After the seller leaves the shop, a policeman enters with a warning to watch for a stolen, three-thousand-dollar fur coat. If the coat is found in a pawnshop, it will carry a penalty of five years in jail for the pawnshop owner.

The partners are terrified and give the coat to the next customer as a gift with her purchase of just a ten-cent thermos bottle. Within moments of this customer's departure from the shop, the policeman returns to tell them the coat was found. Immediately the man who pawned the fur coat returns for it. The owners are in trouble and bickering as the play ends.

This unproduced sketch led to another Kaufman/Mankiewicz collaboration, *The Good Fellow,* which opened on 5 October 1926, at the Playhouse Theatre in New York. It closed after a week of performances. This play and *Fancy Meeting You Again,* written with Leueen MacGrath in 1952, both share the dubious distinction of being the briefest Broadway runs accorded to plays by Kaufman.

The Good Fellow is a spoof on the fraternal orders that were becoming increasingly popular for men from all walks of life. These groups with their secret rituals, backslapping comradeship, and dedication to organizational goals provided a prime target for the satiric skills of Kaufman and Mankiewicz.

Jim Helton, the perennial joiner, comes home from the annual convention of his lodge—Grand National Encampment of the Ancient Order of Corsicans—that was held in Atlantic City, New Jersey. He has managed to have his town of Wilkes-Barre, Pennsylvania, designated as the site of the next annual convention, by promising to raise ten thousand dollars of support money for the convention. As usual, his real estate business and family life will be placed second to his lodge activities.

Act 2 takes place a month later. Helton's fund-raising attempts have proven unsuccessful, but he is determined to succeed. He secretly borrows five thousand dollars against his life insurance policy, and the remaining money is acquired from rich, young Mr. Drayton, the boyfriend of Helton's daughter Ethel. Drayton donates the money on the condition that the contribution remains anonymous. That evening the Wilkes-Barre chapter of the Ancient Order of Corsicans meets in full regalia at Helton's home. The rituals of the lodge are performed with Helton presiding; he is flushed with success, which is short-lived. Ethel, upon becoming engaged to Drayton, accidentally learns of her father's deal with him. She returns home in a state of agitation and breaks up the lodge meeting. Ethel declares she can never marry Drayton because of her father's behavior. Mrs. Helton suddenly realizes that Helton borrowed money against his life insurance policy. Helton is in deep trouble as the meeting dissolves.

The family wounds have not healed overnight, and during act 3, which takes place the next morning, Ethel announces she is moving to Philadelphia. Drayton arrives and persuades her of his devotion and desire to marry her. He also offers Helton the new position as head of the Welfare Department for the miners working at the Pittston and Wilkes-Barre Coal Company. The offer carries the contingency that Helton must resign from his lodge. Helton refuses to accept the offer, but several of his lodge buddies arrive to tell him that they are no longer interested in continuing as lodge members. As a result of the failure of the lodge, Helton accepts Drayton's offer. Happiness seems to have settled upon the household. But the morning mail brings a new lodge temptation to place in Helton's path.

The ending to this play illustrates how hard Kaufman worked to avoid predictable, sentimental conclusions. His concluding solutions were often overworked and emotionally dissatisfying for the audience, but his message is clear: a deep-seated problem can not be cured by a sentimental fix. Helton's addiction could not be controlled by a mere promise to comply with the wishes of his family. This general message and the antisentimental pattern for the final moment of action are used repeatedly in Kaufman's plays throughout the decades.

While the theme of *The Good Fellow* is amusing, even sixty years after it first appeared, the script is uneven. Sometimes the dialogue is too wordy and the situation becomes heavy-handed, particularly in the third act when it ceases to be humorous. The family crisis is an emotional one, and Helton is so fatuous that he loses credibility. When the play was originally staged, it may have encountered another problem: undoubtedly many male audience members were insulted by the barbs and buffoonery since they may have been dedicated members of fraternal orders.

A tour of the play was out of the question, but Paramount Pictures acquired the film rights. For an undiscovered reason the studio did not make a film until 1943, when it released the movie as *Good Fellows.*

Despite Kaufman's problems with Mankiewicz's work habits and their failed effort as collaborators, in 1942 Kaufman allowed Mankiewicz to talk him into another joint venture—writing a screenplay. The weak script, *Sleeper Jump,* never sold, and Mankiewicz had neither mended his poor working habits nor cured his dependency on alcohol. Kaufman should have known better than to attempt another endeavor with his former assistant, who had been working in Hollywood since 1926. But the successful playwright seemed unable to refuse entreaties from friends to collaborate with him. The lesson was not new to Kaufman, and it was one he never seemed to learn.

A War Set to Music

Prior to beginning work on *The Royal Family,* Kaufman was commissioned by Edgar Selwyn, an established producer, to write the book for a musical with a score by George and Ira Gershwin. The writing began on "Strike Up the Band" during the spring of 1926, when Kaufman developed two themes for the script: the self-serving concerns of businessmen, which he had used previously, and the folly of war, a new theme for him.

Horace J. Fletcher of the Fletcher American Cheese Company wants the United States government to maintain a fifty percent tariff on imported cheese. Colonel Holmes, who is the confidential adviser to the president of the United States, arrives at the cheese company to discuss the tariff situation with Fletcher. They conclude that a refusal to repeal the tariff may lead to war with Switzerland. After a series of absurd political insults, war is declared between the two countries. Woven into this plot are two young couples who fall in love, a love interest between Holmes and a widow, an ambitious cheese-factory employee who is also prone to jealousy, and a mysterious chameleon—Mr. Spelvin.

The war is run by Fletcher, who holds the title of Brigadier-Chairman of the Board of Directors. Upon arriving in Switzerland, the scene of the war zone, Fletcher decides the war must be concluded by the end of the week because it is losing money for him. Since American soldiers have never engaged in a battle with the Swiss military, who are evasive, it is impossible to ascertain a victory. Fletcher names Spelvin general for a day with the enjointure that he "show results to hold the job." Spelvin must victoriously end the war that day to be successful.

The love entanglements surface again in the second act, since the group visiting the troops includes the female half of each couple. Also threaded throughout the act is the spoofing of army life. The plot begins to wend its way toward a reconciliation when Jim, the hero who is a conscripted soldier, tells Spelvin how to win the war in one action. Spelvin follows Jim's instructions, and the Americans are victorious. The spy/villain (jealous employee) of the story is unmasked; Spelvin's true identity is revealed—he is in the American Secret Service; and love conquers all for the two romantic couples.

In act 3 everyone returns to the United States, and just as the victory is being celebrated, another tariff situation—this time with Russia—looms on the horizon. Peace will not be permanent since business and trade rather than goodwill toward humanity govern the world.

The ending of this play has a feeling comparable to the conclusion of *The Good Fellow*. At the moment when the situation seems resolved, a similar event or new temptation arises to signal that the general problem is not solvable. "Strike Up the Band" shows that man's greed and his warring tendencies can not be curbed by either tricks or guile.

"Strike Up the Band" began its out-of-town tryouts in Long Branch, New Jersey, on 29 August 1927. From there it went to Philadelphia, where its scheduled six-week run ended after two weeks since it drew very small audiences. The Broadway opening was canceled. Even so, producer Selwyn maintained that the show had potential, and he believed the book could work if it was less biting in its satire. Within two years Selwyn proposed a new production of "Strike Up the Band." Kaufman had no desire to rewrite the book of his second out-of-town failure, so Morrie Ryskind, a colleague of Kaufman's, was contracted to revise the book. Kaufman received credit as author of the original book; Ryskind's version of *Strike Up the Band* opened on 14 January, 1930 and ran for 191 performances.

Kaufman's 1927 script failed for a number of reasons. The public was not enthusiastic about a musical story line with a depressing outlook. The theater public was becoming increasingly affluent. There was continued optimism that World War I had ended wars for all time. The economic woes of the Great Depression were as undreamed of as were the international political crises of the 1930s. Kaufman's humorously cynical look at how man instigates war in a frivolous, selfish manner proved too biting. While war-profiteering, absurd militarism, and misguided patriotism are unpleasant topics, it is fascinating to see how comically they are treated. Unfortunately in act 2 the plot replete with subplots and characters fell victim to the satire. The social and political barbs caused some critics to compare "Strike Up the Band" to the operettas composed by the renowned English team of Gilbert and Sullivan.

Kaufman continued to cling to his job on the *New York Times* with its salary of eighty dollars per week, specifically because he neither believed in his ability nor in his luck to keep succeeding as a Broadway playwright. Undoubtedly, *The Good Fellow* and "Strike Up the Band" reinforced his feeling that failure was always imminent.

Another Romp with the Marx Brothers

The Marx Brothers were ready for another Broadway stint. Sam H. Harris asked Kaufman to create the book for a new musical production with lyrics and music by Bert Kalmar and Harry Ruby. Kaufman began *Animal Crackers* with Morrie Ryskind as his collaborator. Ryskind, who had served as Kaufman's assistant on *The Cocoanuts* primarily as a cut-and-rewrite person on the out-of-town run of the production, was a journalist whose speciality was comic verse. The authors set to work utilizing the pattern for action Kaufman had created for *The Cocoanuts.* They fashioned conventional, relatively shallow characters who operate in a setting that lends itself to formal rules of deportment. The three Marx clowns (Zeppo was the exception) could indulge in their established acts of buffoonery within the prescribed environment—Groucho hurtling his puns, Harpo breaking social rules, and Chico creating chaos.

Mrs. Rittenhouse, a dowager, is hosting a weekend party at her Long Island mansion with the hope that it will be considered the social event of the season. She has gone out of her way to invite such prominent guests as the African explorer Captain Spalding (Groucho), a major financier named Mr. Chandler who is a lover of art, and various persons representing the arts and the social world. Two musicians hired to play at the event are Emanuel Ravelli (Chico) and the Professor (Harpo). Jamison (Zeppo) is Captain Spalding's aide-de-camp.

All of Mrs. Rittenhouse's plans go awry: The painting she arranged to preview is stolen by envious socialites; Arabelle, Mrs. Rittenhouse's daughter, falls in love with a gossip columnist who is covering the weekend party; reputations are at stake rather than being made; and chaos reigns much of the time. Eventually the various strands of the plot are resolved.

Obviously the insane plot merely provides the vehicle for merriment. The reviewers are positive, but mention the lack of innovativeness that was usually expected from Kaufman's work. Pierre de Rohan of the *New York American* comments that "there is nothing startling or revolutionary in the new play. As a matter of fact, it is new only in name and in such relatively minor details as music, plot, and setting."

Obviously de Rohan has detected the pattern for characterization and the set bits of stage business (*lazzi*) performed by each Marx brother. The reviewer for the *New York Times* (24 October 1928) summarizes the script for *Animal Crackers* as "uncommonly perfunctory in its construction as a musical entertainment." The production, which opened 23 October 1928, was successful at the box office and had a run of 213 performances. A film with the screenplay written by Morrie Ryskind was made in 1930.

Kaufman the Director

Kaufman, at age thirty-nine, embarked on a third career as a director of plays. Jed Harris, who planned to produce a play by former Chicago journalists Ben Hecht and Charles MacArthur, offered Kaufman the opportunity to direct this play. There were several reasons why Harris believed that Kaufman was his best choice. The script needed to be reworked, and Kaufman had the reputation of being the best cutter and fastest rewriter in theater; Kaufman had newspaper experience so his sense of detail would enhance the believability of the production about two reporters from Chicago; and the play, titled *The Front Page,* had dialogue that is brisk, lively, and energetic, and therefore similar in style to Kaufman's plays. The play opened on Broadway on 14 August 1928 and had a profitable run of 276 performances.

Kaufman's career as a director spanned nearly thirty years. He directed forty-three productions including John Steinbeck's *Of Mice and Men* (1937), Jerome Chodorov and Joseph Field's *My Sister Eileen* (1940), Abe Burrow and Jo Swerling's *Guys and Dolls* (1950), and Peter Ustinov's *Romanoff and Juliet* (1957). After directing his own play, *June Moon,* in 1929, he always desired to be the director for his scripts since it gave him control over the interpretation of the script and more of a voice in other production aspects. Therefore, among Kaufman's many directorial credits are twenty-three of his own plays. His boundless energy coupled with his multifaceted talents obviously enabled him to maintain a trifurcated career in the waning years of the decade.

A Busy 1929

Kaufman wrote a sketch with Ryskind in April 1929 that was submitted for copyright at the same time as was *Animal Crackers.* The sketch *Something New,* which may have been produced for one of

Kaufman's professional clubs, is a spoof on both the drama of Eugene O'Neill and the use of the flashback. The celebrated O'Neill was frequently a target of Kaufmanian barbs inserted casually into the dialogue of a play. O'Neill's pre-eminence among American dramatists and his psychological dramas made him perfect for comic deflation.

The plot of *Something New* is built on the desire of a dying old man to share his secret with his two grandchildren. The grandfather's tale results in three flashback scenes that are a composite of three separate melodramatic moments, which are not related to each other except they each feature a man. In the brief final moment of the play the old man concludes the tale, "And that, my dears, is the story of why your grandmother and I—never married." The sequence of the plot actually makes no sense since it is impossible to determine why he never married. Laurence Shyer dubs this script a "Nonsense Play" in his 1978 *Theatre* magazine article.[19]

Also in 1929 Kaufman worked separately with two new collaborators, Ring Lardner and Alexander Woollcott, who were friends of his and Algonquin regulars. The play with Lardner was the first of these projects to get started. Lardner's 1921 short story "Some Like Them Cold" appealed to Kaufman, who proposed that they adapt it for the stage. Work on this project began early in 1929, when Lardner wrote the first draft. Kaufman read it and made suggestions for changes. They handled each following draft with the same procedure.[20] By the end of the summer the play *June Moon* went into rehearsal with Kaufman directing this comic, satiric account of how popular songs are composed, published, and pushed in Tin Pan Alley—the district in New York City associated at that time with musicians, composers, and publishers of popular music.

June Moon opens with a prologue set in a train parlor car taking Fred M. Stevens, a young, naive songwriter, to New York City where he is hoping to launch his career. Fred begins to talk to another passenger, Edna Baker, who becomes his first friend in New York City. Act 1 takes place about ten days later, when Fred is invited to the apartment of a once-successful songwriter named Paul Sears. Sears has not recently written a hit song; he hopes Fred's lyrics will help to reestablish his reputation with new hits. Sears introduces Fred to his sister-in-law Eileen, who is the sister of Fred's wife Lucille, a wisecracking, unsatisfied woman. Fred is taken with Eileen's big-city look and manner; he begins to forget his attachment to Edna.

Several weeks later Sears and Fred are meeting at Gobel's music publishing house to present Mr. Hart with their first song titled "June Moon." When the song is purchased by the publisher, an excited Fred forgets Edna, who is in an outer waiting area expecting news of the audition results. Fred instead joins Sears, his wife, and Eileen to celebrate their success. Eileen lavishes cordiality on Fred after she discovers that her former beau (Hart) has a new romantic interest.

Within a month, life has taken a few new twists for Fred. He is engaged to Eileen, and the wedding is to take place in three days. "June Moon" is becoming a successful song, and the team of Sears and Stevens is busy trying to write more hits. Fred is distracted from his work, however, by Eileen's money-spending habits and her general manner. Eventually circumstances and the assistance of friends help Fred to realize that Eileen is not right for him, but the devoted Edna is the ideal woman. The play concludes with a sense of future happiness and success for Fred and Edna.

June Moon opened on Broadway on 9 October 1929, and ran throughout the season for 272 performances. A road company opened in Chicago during the Broadway run, another company went on tour after the show closed in New York, and the play became a popular piece for theater companies in the 1930s. Film rights were sold to Paramount, which released *June Moon* in 1931. In 1937 another film version was released with the title *Blond Trouble.* The Manhattan Punch Line Theatre staged a successful revival of the play during its 1983–84 season.

Lardner—known primarily as a short-story writer but also as a humorist and satirist—had previously failed as a playwright. He worked diligently on *June Moon,* despite failing health. Lardner had a preference for popular music and enjoyed composing songs; he wrote the words and music for the four songs in *June Moon*: two love songs—the title song and "Montana Moon," plus two novelty numbers—"Hello Tokio" and a lament of an unwed mother.

The reviewers lauded *June Moon,* but the *New York Times* review (10 October 1929) is a bit more circumspect in assessing the play: "After the first act the story becomes conventional and the enjoyment lies in the broadness of the comedy." It was the domesticities revealed at the apartment of Paul Sears in act 1 that the reviewer believed spoke of "the moderns who live with 'quiet desperation,' selfish and thwarted, hard, calculating, disloyal." The play loses its intimate focus after act

1 when it becomes more involved in examining the workings of life on Tin Pan Alley. Once again, the wit and satire in acts 2 and 3 dominate character evolution and plot development.

June Moon incorporates a technique for changing the flow of dialogue that Kaufman had perfected over the previous five years. He first used simultaneous dialogue—several characters speaking at the same time—in *Beggar on Horseback*. He introduces the device either to punctuate the subtext of the script or to heighten a moment. In act 1 of *June Moon* the first example of this technique occurs toward the end of the act when Eileen is talking on the telephone to Hart while Maxie is leaving Paul and Fred. Eileen's conversation is based on her reaction to lies Hart is telling her because he wants to end their relationship. Meanwhile, the dialogue between the men repeatedly uses "good-by" and "goodnight." It is almost like a choral chant reminiscent of classical Greek drama, and it is Kaufman's sophisticated usage of the overlapping dialogue technique.

The other example of overlapping dialogue heightens the excitement of the moment, when it comes at the end of the act: Paul, Lucille, and Eileen are about to take Fred on the town. The dozen short lines asking questions, making remarks about state of readiness, and bursting with commentary about the enjoyment that awaits the quartet fill the moment with gaiety and expectation. This technique also serves to buoy a slightly hesitant Fred out the door.

The success of *June Moon* delighted Lardner, but he did not cope well with it. He returned to his drinking bouts, and his health continued to fail. In the early 1930s Kaufman and Lardner began work on a second endeavor: the subject of the script was alcoholism. Unfortunately Lardner's death on 24 September 1933, came before he finished drafting the script.

The other partnership that Kaufman began in the summer of 1929 was with Alexander Woollcott, who spoke of wanting to collaborate on a play with his friend and former assistant at the *New York Times*. The script was to be an adaptation of a short story called "Boule de Suif" by Guy de Maupassant. The play, titled "The Channel Road," takes place in the main room of a roadside inn in Normandy, and the story is generally concerned with the Prussian occupation of France during the winter of 1870. Specifically the plot presents a situation in which a prostitute is cast into a difficult moral dilemma. Supposedly Woollcott was extremely fascinated with the harlot in literature; thus, he selected the material for the script.

Pierre, the wounded son of Widow Beauvais, returns to her inn after his army unit suffers defeat on the battlefield. He discovers that the inn is inhabited by the enemy, Prussian officers, who are quartered there until a treaty is signed. A coachload of seven French citizens from Rouen arrives; they are going to Havre under safe conduct permits. Six of the passengers—two nuns, two ladies, and their related gentlemen—are discomfited by the presence of the seventh passenger, Madeleine Rousset, a notorious prostitute from their city. Rousset claims to have strangled a Prussian soldier when he entered her famed house. Lieutenant Engel, the Prussian officer in charge of the inn and the surrounding countryside, is attracted to Mlle Rousset. She refuses his advances, and all the travelers are detained as a result.

The following morning the lieutenant continues to hold the Havre-bound party. Several of the travelers believe Rousset should satisfy the lieutenant so the journey can proceed. During a Christmas Eve party the travelers befriend Rousset in order to persuade her to appease the officer. When idealistic Pierre returns to the inn, he is greatly disappointed to learn of Rousset's capitulation.

Christmas morning finds the travelers once more ignoring Rousset as they plan their departure. She tries to explain to Pierre her reasons for finally acquiescing to the officer's demand. This situation alters Pierre's attitude from dissolution to anger at his fellow citizens who take, but desire not to give.

The play opened on 17 October, eight days after *June Moon* and eleven days before 29 October when the stock market crashed, thereby ushering in the era of the Great Depression for the United States. The play was not a success with either the public or the critics; it closed after sixty performances. However, given the economic situation in the country as well as mixed reviews, this was not a bad run for any play at that particular moment in American history.

The deficiencies of the script were laid at Woollcott's feet since his style was so discernible. The morning following the opening of the play Robert Littell wrote that the play "remains a short story, and one notices in it too many places that were thin and stretched in the process of extending it into a play. And so one must confess to some disappointment at the very first play of Alexander Woollcott."[21]

Noted critic Joseph Wood Krutch, in writing an evaluation of American drama from 1918 to 1939, states, "and the nostalgic sentimentality of "The Channel Road" is such pure Alexander Woollcott that Mr. Kaufman can have contributed nothing except his technical skill."[22] There is little of Kaufman's style in the work to ascribe it to him.

Kaufman's forte was writing plays set in contemporary America. "The Channel Road" forced him to work with a foreign setting as well as a historical period, just as "Jacques Duval, M.D." had. Both plays lack the rich cultural details that permeate other Kaufman plays.

The style of the language was immediately detected by reviewers as belonging to Woollcott for it was florid, studied, and bombastic. Francis R. Bellamy of *Outlook* comments that while the characters may look like de Maupassant's people their voices are "the voice of Mr. Woollcott, talking brightly to himself. . . ."[23] Kaufman had given in to Woollcott's ideas on choice of material, language, and the sentimental tone. The reasons for Kaufman's capitulation are unknown, but intimidation by his former boss, or his busy schedule—particularly as it related to *June Moon,* or the overwhelming personality of Woollcott are obvious elements that may have contributed.

The decade ended on a note of financial disaster for many of the Algonquin Wits who had made their marks during the heydays of the roaring twenties. But Kaufman's resources were not a worry to him. He would be sustained by royalties from his numerous copyrights, future box office successes that he would write in the 1930s, and his work as a director. Kaufman progressed, during the twenties, from a struggling playwright to a successful and influential man of American theater.

Chapter Four
The Early Thirties

As the new decade began George S. Kaufman was engaged in collaboration with Moss Hart, Kaufman's first non-Algonquin partner on a full-length play. The new playwriting team began work at a time when the Algonquin group was slowly dispersing. Many of the members, particularly the writers of the Vicious Circle who had gained fame and fortune during the twenties, were retreating to their recently acquired country homes and were, therefore, unavailable for lunches and other social gatherings in the city. Marriage failures within the group caused additional strains, and the 1929 Wall Street crash—more than any single factor—dampened the spirit of the Round Tablers. In the early thirties several of the members moved to Southern California while others, including Kaufman, became frequent West-Coast visitors. Then in 1931, when the *World* newspaper stopped publishing, the scattering of the Algonquin Wits became even more evident. Many members of the group had worked for this publication. Margaret Case Harriman observes that "the Algonquin Round Table did not die suddenly: it faded away as imperceptibly as it had come in to being. Even its own members were not conscious that it was drawing to a close."[1] Surely Kaufman, whose work load had increased toward the end of the twenties due to his three career paths—his *New York Times* position, playwriting, and directing—hardly had time to participate in two-hour Round Table lunches.

Despite the fact that the 1930–31 theater season came toward the end of the first full year of the Great Depression, and business on Broadway was at an all-time low, Kaufman and Hart's play *Once in a Lifetime* was a sensational hit. Kaufman's playwriting and directing talents remained as much in demand as ever, even in the face of national economic disaster.

A Modern Revue

During the first eight months of 1930, while Kaufman was revising and rehearsing *Once in a Lifetime,* he was also conferring with Morrie

Ryskind on a satiric musical concerned with American politics. This project moved into the scenario phase by fall, was then given to the Gershwins to begin their score, and eventually was shelved until the summer of 1931. Meanwhile Kaufman, who was acting in the Broadway cast of *Once in a Lifetime,* was asked by Howard Dietz to collaborate on writing all the sketches for a new Max Gordon revue. Dietz planned to write all the lyrics, and Arthur Schwartz agreed to compose all the music. Kaufman accepted the offer to work on this project since Dietz's approach to creating this revue was different from the usual method, which was to take sketches and music created by a number of different talented people, thereby trusting to luck when assembling the diverse pieces into a show. The objective behind Dietz's approach was to create a revue with a planned unity.

The Band Wagon, which opened on 3 June 1931, was considered to be the sophisticated revue of the 1931–32 season. Brooks Atkinson in his enthusiastic *New York Times* review (5 June 1931) hails this revue as "beginning a new era." He considers it a thoroughly modern revue. "It is both funny and lovely; it has wit, gaiety, and splendor." He comments several paragraphs later that it contains "no devastating wise-cracks, no smutty jokes, no heavy-handed gags and no laboriously assembled jests—the satire is adroit, informed, and intelligent. You need not check your brains with your hat."

The revue included six Kaufman and Dietz sketches plus two monologues. The latter pieces were performed by comedian Frank Morgan, while nearly everyone in the cast—including dancing stars Fred and Adele Astaire—performed in the sketches. "When the Rain Goes Pitter-Patter" concerns the dilemma of two theater goers who are unsuccessful in their attempts to hail a taxi on a wet night. "For Good Old Nector" introduces what would happen to university spirit and pride if more emphasis were put on studying than on football. "The Pride of the Claghornes" turns the most hallowed traditions of the South topsy-turvy. "Still Again" is a takeoff of a convicted murderer's last five minutes of life while he continues to hope for a gubernatorial reprieve. "The Great Warburton Mystery" is a witty satire on fictional detectives' methods of solving a murder. "Pour Le Bain" applies sophisticated salesmanship techniques toward a shy female customer for the marketing of bathroom fixtures.

These brief plot descriptions indicate that the sketches are topical, and that they cover various subjects based on the American life-style. However the subject matter is definitely free of any associations that would remind the 1931 audience of either the national economy or the political scene.

Bolstered by rave newspaper reviews, *The Band Wagon* ran for 262 performances and established Max Gordon as an important producer. Gordon was delighted about this first professional association with Kaufman, and he would on numerous occasions, in succeeding years, work with the playwright. Another measure of success was that two films were inspired by the revue: *Dancing in the Dark* (1949) and *The Band Wagon* (1953). The films discarded the sketches and created screenplays around the songs.

Max Gordon decided to produce another Schwartz/Dietz revue called "Flying Colors" for the 1932–33 season. This was an unfortunate decision for Gordon, who was already facing a deteriorating financial situation. His depression increased due to the lackadaisical quality of his revue. As Gordon's depression grew worse, George S. Kaufman, the play doctor par excellence, hurried to Philadelphia, where the revue was in tryouts, to help mend the show.

Kaufman reworked the dialogue of Dietz's sketches and added new pieces. One of the additions, titled *On the American Plan,* bears the credits "By George S. Kaufman and Howard Dietz." This is a macabre comedy set in the lobby of the Remington Arms Hotel. The hotel is enjoying a booming business because the stock market continues its plummet. Clients are checking into the hotel in order to commit suicide by jumping out of windows, shooting themselves, drowning themselves in the bathtubs, or taking poison. The hotel staff members, who are used to these various routines of self-destruction, are extremely helpful to all the distressed clients. The fifth and last man to register at the hotel is a theatrical producer. When the man tells the desk clerk his occupation, the clerk's line is, "Say no more!" as he hands the producer a gun.

"Flying Colors" opened on 15 September 1932, and ran for 188 performances. Max Gordon recovered from his nervous breakdown and was released from Leroy Sanitarium after the revue had opened to "mild reviews."[2]

Trouble for the Play Doctor

In April 1931, after leaving the cast of *Once in a Lifetime,* Kaufman—who was never one to be idle—had some time between his work with Dietz and his plan to resume work with Ryskind on the musical *Of*

Thee I Sing. As he had in the past, Kaufman reviewed a number of
plays that writer friends, producers, or acquaintances believed his doctoring skills would turn into box office successes. Often his work as
play doctor went unsigned by him; however, he usually received an
author's share of the royalties. He turned a number of promising scripts
into successful plays.

After Kaufman read a number of submitted scripts, his attention
was drawn to "Hot Pan" by Edward J. Eustace, who used the pseudonym Michael Swift. This script, a satiric comedy set in the California
gold rush days and focusing on American greed, had played at the
Provincetown Playhouse for nineteen performances in February.

It seems Kaufman never agreed to rewrite "Hot Pan" with its original author, but suggested Laurence Stallings as his collaborator. According to Goldstein's account of this production,[3] Kaufman and
Stallings reworked the newly titled script "Eldorado" through three
versions. Although still not satisfied with the last revision, Kaufman
persuaded producer Sam Harris to have the play go through the tryout
performance process. The play, with Kaufman and Stallings taking
program credits for both playwriting and codirection, failed in New
Haven during October 1931.

Stalking the Pulitzer Prize

Upon leaving New Haven, Kaufman immediately started rehearsals
for *Of Thee I Sing,* the musical he had started in 1930 with Ryskind.
They resumed work on the book during the summer of 1931, and by
fall they gave the script to the Gershwins, who immediately set to
finishing the score. The musical was mounted for the 1931–32 season.

The plot for *Of Thee I Sing* begins in the midst of an early 1930s
prenominating-convention political campaign rally being staged by
Wintergreen for president. The story then follows John P. Wintergreen's campaign from the nominating convention, where he has been
nominated on the sixty-third ballot, to his triumphant election on the
slogan "Put Love in the White House." Newspaper-king Matthew Ar-
nold Fulton, proposes the idea that becomes the promotional issue of
the presidential campaign: bachelor candidate Wintergreen should fall
in love with a typical American girl. Wintergreen would find the right
woman as a result of a Miss White House contest, and the winner's
grand prize would be to marry Wintergreen. However, after all the
contest hoopla promoted by Fulton, Wintergreen meets and promptly

falls in love with pretty, demure Mary Turner, an employee of Fulton's. Following much trumpery, Wintergreen is elected president. He is then inaugurated and married to Mary at the same time by one of the Chief Justices.

The White House several weeks later is the setting for act 2. There is much ado about Wintergreen's not marrying the winner of the contest who is the jilted, beauteous Miss Devereaux. The French government becomes involved in the situation by claiming that Miss Devereaux, a French descendant, has had her rights trampled in the dust. Wintergreen is faced with either impeachment or abandoning Mary to marry Diana Devereaux when Mary saves the day by announcing she is about to be a mother. The Wintergreens become the proud parents of White House twins, and Devereaux is betrothed to Vice President Throttlebottom at the final curtain. Interwoven throughout the plot is the comic struggle for recognition patiently undertaken by Alexander Throttlebottom, the party's candidate who is elected vice president.

This lampoon of national politics was heralded as "probably the first and surely the best musical satire ever written on American politics."[4] In his review Richard Lockridge notes, "the great generosity of ideas which makes *Of Thee I Sing* so unusual is additional" to the usual attributes of musicals: beautiful girls, lively music, and lovers nearly parted.[5] John Mason Brown joined the many reviewers applauding the quality of the musical: "Here at last is a musical show which dodges nearly all the clichés of its kind, which has wit and intelligence behind it, which brings Gilbert and Sullivan to mind without being derived from them, and which makes hilarious satiric use of the American scene in general and Washington politics in particular."[6] To crown all the compliments, the Pulitzer Prize Committee for drama in May 1932 chose *Of Thee I Sing* as the best play of the season.

This selection was a departure and surprise because the Pulitzer Prize had never before been awarded to a musical script, but was always granted on the basis of literary excellence. As a result of this standard, the music was separated from the script, and the prize was awarded to the creators of the book (Kaufman and Ryskind) and the lyricist (Ira Gershwin). The musical won the award over such competitors as *Mourning Becomes Electra* by Eugene O'Neill, *Reunion in Vienna,* by Robert E. Sherwood, and *The Animal Kingdom* by Phillip Barry.

Several critics editorially debated the committee's decision. Brooks Atkinson both defends and condemns the award being given to a mu-

sical. He contends that the script *Of Thee I Sing* "has applied intelligence to a form of stage writing that has long contented itself with
hackneyed imbecility." The next paragraph cites another defense for
the award: "It honors topical satire in the Broadway vernacular as one
of the liveliest things in the American theatre, and it recognizes
Mr. Kaufman's innumerable achievements in that vein."[7] However, in
the final paragraph of the article, Atkinson labels the Pulitzer committee's judgment as "skittish" for preferring a musical comedy
book—without its music—to several excellent plays. The critical debate only increased the publicity for the show.

Perhaps another opportunity resulting from the Pulitzer Prize was
Knopf's publication of the musical's text and lyrics in book form. This,
too, was a distinction since *Of Thee I Sing* was the first American musical script to be published for the general public. It was an extremely
successful book that had seven printings in 1932.

Of Thee I Sing completed a run of 446 performances. In the ensuing
years various producers offered to mount a revival of the award-winning
musical, always to be turned down by Kaufman. Finally, after twenty
years, a revival was created for the 1951–52 Broadway season starring
Jack Carson as John P. Wintergreen. This production ran only seventy-
two performances. The script did not lend itself to updating: post-
World-War-II politics and international affairs were not readily
shuffled into the 1930s format. A revival of the musical as it was originally conceived has not been professionally staged, but the enduring
accomplishment of the book and score might shine forth if contemporary interest revives nostalgia for the thirties.

A Successful Dinner Party

The idea for Kaufman's next collaboration had been discussed with
Edna Ferber many years before it was finally developed. The idea was
to tell the story of a dinner party from the moment of its planning by
the hostess until the guests go into the dining room for dinner. During
a discussion on New Year's Eve—as 1931 was about to depart—Ferber
reintroduced the *Dinner at Eight* idea, and Kaufman began to warm to
it. Work began on the script in the spring, and it was completed by
June 1932. *Dinner at Eight* opened 22 October 1932 and ran for 243
performances.

Mrs. Millicent Jordan is the organizer of the dinner party for Lord
and Lady Ferncliffe. Upon the Ferncliffes' acceptance of her invitation,

Millicent telephones invitations to people who are eligible and appropriate guests for the nobility. The action of the play skips around New York City, showing the guests in their own environments and beset with their problems.

While Mrs. Jordan is absorbed in the flurry of activities connected with her dinner party, she never becomes aware of the lives around her and their intrigues. She fails to notice that her husband's business is failing and he is suffering from severe heart disease. She does not know that the flamboyant Dan Packard, whom she invited, is secretly acquiring the Jordan family shipping business. She is unaware that Mrs. Packard is involved in a secret amour with Doctor Talbot, another dinner guest and the Jordans' family physician. She does not know that the famous film star Larry Renault, who is to grace her table, is her daughter's lover. He is, for all his grandeur, a penniless alcoholic facing eviction from his hotel. She knows nothing of the marriage and fight taking place among her servants on the day of the dinner.

The guests of honor break their engagement to the Jordans' dinner party, so Millicent invites her middle-class sister and brother-in-law to substitute for the Ferncliffes. All the guests, except Larry Renault—who, unknown to the gathered dinner guests has committed suicide in his hotel room—hear the news of the nobility's defection from the dinner party as they drift off to the dining room, chattering innocuously.

This play was lavishly costumed and sumptuously decorated in order to match the wealth alluded to in the script. The period for the script is Depression-ridden America 1932. Surely Millicent Jordan appeared to be a self-involved, foolish woman. The contrast between the realities of life in the thirties and the realities attributed particularly to the rich, idle female characters in the play make this a powerful social satire. It also provides satiric commentary that contrasts the social practices of the fashionable upper class with the conduct of the Jordans' servants. The play openly displays the disillusionment, the decadence, and the vanity at work behind the facade of wealth. Even Eleanor Flexner, who constantly chips away at the Kaufman reputation, claims: "The futility, emptiness, and self-interest which go with a certain degree of social decay and wealth have never been more damningly depicted."[8] But she is disappointed in *Dinner at Eight* because the authors did not include "a sense of outrage, a scale of values, a point of view."[9] Does she expect a play to do too much? It seems that Kaufman and Ferber's point of view is obvious, but the play presents a keen observation of social issues and practices rather than trying to offer Band-Aid remedies.

Brooks Atkinson generally addresses the same issues in his *New York Times* review of 24 October 1932: "Although it is lightened with humor, it is a reflective drama, detached and observant." *Dinner at Eight* presents a basically serious theme, and Atkinson considered it to be Kaufman and Ferber's most ambitious play. But he faulted the work for its ironic and incomplete final scene. He desired, as did a few other critics, to view the dinner party in action as the last image. This critical controversy neither interfered with business at the box office nor with a subsequent film sale to Metro-Goldwyn-Mayer.

The screenplay was written by Herman J. Mankiewicz in collaboration with Frances Marion. The film has an all-star cast including Billie Burke, Jean Harlow, John Barrymore, Marie Dressler, Lionel Barrymore, and Wallace Beery, a casting that represents the first time six stars appeared in the same motion picture. The 1933 film directed by George Cukor is still a memorable cinematic experience. It may be the best film ever made from a script bearing Kaufman's name.

More Musicals

While 1932 only brought forth one new major script by Kaufman, *Variety* reported in the 29 November 1932 issue that "George S. Kaufman is figured to be the biggest money maker on Broadway this season. He's getting over $7000—may be its eight G's every week—more than any manager is earning, probably including Sam H. Harris who produced a trio of shows which George wrote and staged and has a piece of."

The years 1933 and 1934 marked Kaufman's return to creating at least two new plays per season. *Let 'Em Eat Cake* is the musical sequel to *Of Thee I Sing,* and it opened on 21 October 1933. The book was written by Kaufman and Ryskind, lyrics by Ira Gershwin, and score by George Gershwin.

The plot begins when John P. Wintergreen is running for reelection as president of the United States against John P. Tweedledee. On election night, since Tweedledee wins, Wintergreen and his cohorts are forced to think of another way of earning a living. They decide to go into blue-shirt manufacturing. Mary Wintergreen had inspired the idea for the product named the "Maryblue" shirt. Once the business is started, it fails like every other business in the country. Wintergreen decides a revolution is necessary to improve economic and international conditions. Since the uniform of the revolution becomes the "Mary-blue" shirt, business at the factory begins to boom. This turn of events means America is represented by Wintergreen's Maryblue shirts, while Italy is known for the black shirts of Mussolini, and Germany for the brown shirts of Hitler. The Wintergreen new American revolution eventually succeeds.

Act 2 opens in the Blue House, formerly called the White House. Wintergreen is once more head of state, but this time he is a dictator who will not have to run for reelection. Mary is actively forming a new DAR to instigate the vital reforms related to new rules for playing contract bridge. War-debt problems begin to create unrest, and in an attempt to settle the situation quickly, Wintergreen organizes a base-ball game, the outcome being the deciding factor for whether the former United States allies repay their debts. The teams represent the League of Nations and the United States. Throttlebottom is designated the umpire, but he makes an unpopular call against the U.S. team, and payment of the debt is lost. This time Wintergreen and his friends are caught in the dictatorial web. Instead of merely losing an election, they are convicted by a Tribunal and sentenced to death by guillotine. Once again Mary saves the situation and the life of her husband by staging a revolution to remove the dictator and restore the republic.

The story is complex and confusing; the satire is undisciplined and bitter; and the stage armies seem to be frequently waving their guns. Atkinson concludes in his 23 October 1933, *New York Times* review: "When the long, fierce evening is over you are surprised that so much brilliance can leave such a heavy impression." Fifty-three years later a sour heaviness engulfs one after reading the book. The satire is hard-hitting and uncompromising in its political views. Without the visual spectacle, music, and performance, the mood of the piece may take on even more intensity than it would on stage.

Anticipation for the sequel to the Pulitzer Prize winner *Of Thee I Sing* had been extremely high, but a dissatisfied first-night audience and modest reviews resulted in audiences growing smaller and smaller. Thus the sequel did not enjoy the success of the original, and *Let 'Em Eat Cake* closed after eighty-nine performances. A tour followed after the Broadway closing, but it failed to recoup the weekly expenses. Overhead was high on this production due to a cast of 125 persons plus musicians and stagehands. There was hardly any money left for taxes and other operating expenses after salaries and royalties were paid. The tour was short-lived, and *Let 'Em Eat Cake* is hardly remembered.

Although Kaufman and Ryskind had erred in judging the tolerance of their audiences for *Let 'Em Eat Cake,* they soon tackled another political satire as their sixth association. This script, their first nonmusical play was titled "Bring on the Girls." It sounded like a frolicsome musical and was planned for the 1934–35 Broadway season.

"Bring on the Girls" is a spoof on the Reconstruction Finance Corporation (RFC), a governmental agency established in 1932 to provide loans to financial, industrial, and agricultural institutions. The prologue introduces Jim Pearson and Charlie Meredith, who are completing five-year terms in a federal penitentiary. Jim and Charlie claim they were the first bankers in 1929 to be imprisoned. Before being released from prison, the two men are visited by Crawford, a Justice Department agent with iron-gray hair, who warns them to go straight. Act 1 finds Jim and Charlie in New York City, contacting Charlie's former chorus girl love, Rosemary. Everyone is without money and work; however, Jim hits upon an idea to acquire a little railroad company in order to get federal assistance. A partnership is formed between Jim, Charlie, Rosemary, and her chorus girl roommate Nancy, with the intention of petitioning the RFC for money. The girls are an important part of the plan since they are the bait for the federal agents.

Act 2 takes place a week later. The partnership has acquired the Black Creek Railroad, which runs a distance of two miles from Black Creek, Ohio, to East Black Creek. Three teams of two agents each from the RFC visit the New York apartment office of the railroad and grant the railroad owners a total of four hundred million dollars to support the poor company. The agents are enamored of the beautiful female owners and stay to assist the ladies in their shopping spree. Soon Crawford visits the railroad company office with intention to prove that the partnership should not have received the federal funding since they do not own the railroad. Prior to Crawford's arrival, Jim has been informed that the Black Creek Railroad was taken from him due to unpaid taxes. Quickly Jim informs Crawford that the railroad partnership is a farming institution. Crawford vows to return.

The Black Creek Farm has been in operation for five days when Act 3 commences. Rosemary's apartment and its roof area is the site of intensive farming. Live animals have been purchased, and the six agents who have become part of the menage have helped to establish signs of farm life. This bucolic setting is disturbed by another visit from Crawford, who brings two professors to investigate the farm. Crawford decides that the RFC men are going to jail for the misuse of government funds, and the members of the partnership will be imprisoned since they do not run a legitimate farm business. Despite Jim's eloquent defense of the partnership's pioneering farm efforts, Crawford is about to take the group to jail when a committee reputedly appointed by the mayor of New York City arrives to honor the partnership. The committee claims that Jim and the Black Creek Farm partnership has stimulated the economy of the city, which has returned to prosperity due to the company's farm activities and buying sprees. Jim is presented with a scroll. The professors agree with the Black Creek Farm's achievements as outlined by the mayor's committee, and Crawford loses his case. Upon Crawford's departure, general jubilation breaks out when Jim is reminded by the "Mayor's committee" that he owes each of them five dollars apiece for their performance.

At the conclusion of the play, the audience who has been in on the game throughout realizes that it, too, has been duped. This trick resolution to an inconsequential plot creates a fizzling effect at the end of the performance. The characters are one-dimensional, the situation is absurd, the villain is Jim, the hero who fails to be endearing, and though the failings of the RFC are never defined, the agency is ridiculed because of its general policy. Not even popular radio comedian Jack Benny, who was hired to play his first stage role as Jim Pearson, was able to save "Bring on the Girls" from poor out-of-town reviews.

After the 22 October 1934 opening at the National Theatre in Washington, D.C., the authors spent two weeks trying to improve the unwieldy script. The tryout location moved to New Haven in November, but it still received unexcited notices. Two more rewrites followed two more tryout cities before producer Sam Harris finally closed the show in Hartford on 15 December and canceled all plans for a New York opening.

Kaufman and Ryskind did not collaborate on another Broadway production, but early in 1935 they went to Hollywood to create a Marx Brothers film, *A Night at the Opera,* for producer Irving Thalberg at Metro-Goldwyn-Mayer. This screenplay became Kaufman and Ryskind's last joint effort. Ryskind spent the next eleven years primarily writing screenplays.

A Fling with Mystery

During the same period Kaufman was committed to Ryskind to finish *Let 'Em Eat Cake,* and to film producer Samuel Goldwyn to write his first screenplay. Kaufman again collaborated with Alexander Woollcott. The project for the 1933–34 season with Woollcott, titled *The Dark Tower,* concerns the manipulation of one person's mind by an evil individual, and a murder that will never be solved by the police. Woollcott had a reputation for his fascination with unsolved murder cases, and the idea for the plot was his.

This three-act melodrama opens when actress Jessica Wells and her actor brother Damon return home after appearing in a new play titled "The Dark Tower." They are greeted by Aunt Martha, her serving woman Hattie, and Ben Weston, a theater manager who loves Jessica. Everyone is feeling a bubbling happiness because Jessica has recently recovered from an unknown sorrow and is triumphantly reestablishing her theatrical career. The festive atmosphere is dispelled, however, when Jessica's estranged husband Stanley Vance unexpectedly arrives at Aunt Martha's home. The family had been informed that Stanley had died, but he was actually serving time in prison. Jessica immediately falls, once more, under Stanley's hypnotic power, and he begins to rule her activities.

A week later Vance continues to rule Jessica who has become unable to perform on stage. Vance needs money in order to go to Europe, so he decides to sell Jessica's percentage of "The Dark Tower." He makes arrangements to meet with Max Sarnoff, a prospective buyer, at the Waldorf-Astoria Hotel. With Jessica in tow, Stanley arrives at Sarnoff's hotel suite. Sarnoff arranges to have Jessica dispatched home, and then he serves Vance a drugged cocktail. Once Vance is unconscious, Sarnoff drags him into the closet, stabs him, and locks the body inside.

Sarnoff mysteriously disappears from the boat on which he departed, leaving the police baffled by the events. Jessica begins to recover from her automatous state after Vance's death, which makes Weston think that she was somehow involved in Vance's murder. When Weston shares his fears with Damon, the latter invites Weston to visit their house the next day at 6 p.m. Upon Weston's arrival, he is surprised to be greeted by Sarnoff, who recounts the events of Vance's death and slowly reveals himself to be Damon in disguise. Weston is satisfied that Jessica had no part in the murder, and he plans to take her to Europe so she can fully recover. Damon had been so clever in his disguise that it is evident the police will never solve the murder of evil Stanley Vance.

It appears that staging a merry murder and expecting the audience to react to it with laughter was a misjudgment. Also, the end of the play leaves the audience in a moralistic dilemma. Other weaknesses of the script include its length, a number of dull segments, and unresolved minor plot details. There are a few entertaining scenes that appealed to reviewers and audiences, so the notices in the newspapers were mixed. Brooks Atkinson's review in the *New York Times* (27 November 1933) claims the playwrights "have composed an amiable and amateurish charade which has a good deal of story-book flavor and no more mystery than you need for a genial evening away from home." In his concluding paragraph Atkinson contends *"The Dark Tower* has accordingly a pleasant appearance and a jovial manner. But it has more time at its disposal than most theatergoers have."

The production ran for fifty-seven performances, which was three less than "The Channel Road." A film sale resulted in a 1934 movie titled *The Man with Two Faces* released by First National. But the best and lasting result of having created *The Dark Tower* was that Bennett Cerf, head of a new publishing firm named Random House, chose the script as one of the first dramatic texts the company would publish. This led to Random House's issuing most of Kaufman's subsequent plays in book form.

While preparing the two 1933–34 Broadway scripts, Kaufman finally succumbed to a Hollywood entreaty that carried terms he could abide with: He could write in the location of his choice and not be tied to a studio cell; he would have fellow Round Tabler Robert E. Sherwood as a collaborator; and their contract for fifty thousand dollars had escape clauses permitting the authors to withdraw after writing either the original story outline or the first draft of the screenplay.

The film was to star Eddie Cantor, and producer Samuel Goldwyn desired a script that placed Cantor's character in ancient Rome. Kaufman and Sherwood created a story line with Cantor as a custodian of a historical museum located in an American town named West Rome. Cantor's character falls asleep, and in the dream sequence he experiences life in ancient Rome. After completing the plot outline and the first draft of the screenplay, Kaufman and Sherwood exercised their escape clause in order to complete their other commitments.

When the film *Roman Scandals* was released in December 1933, the original story was credited to Kaufman and Sherwood. The adaptation was credited to two other writers, but actually there had been four assigned to the project. The film was successful, and Kaufman had earned his first credit as the author of an original screenplay.

Two Plays with and about Ladies

Katharine Dayton was introduced by Ethel Taylor, a play agent, to George S. Kaufman in the early spring of 1934. Dayton was interested in writing a comedy utilizing her knowledge of life in the nation's capital, and Kaufman seemed to be the ideal collaborator for her. After his initial meeting with Dayton at the Algonquin, he agreed to work with her.

Dayton was an intelligent woman with impressive credentials. She had studied to be an actress, but turned to writing as a career. Her first stories appeared in *Vanity Fair* in 1920, and in the next ten years she contributed many articles to the *New York Tribune*. In 1928 she became a Washington correspondent for the North American Newspaper Alliance, an association that she continued until 1935. Dayton also gained a reputation during the period from 1928 to 1937 for her series of humorous articles titled "Mrs. Democrat and Mrs. Republican" which appeared in the *Saturday Evening Post*. It was natural that Dayton and Kaufman would decide to write a satire illustrating how social trivialities may affect political life.

Although the two writers began their collaboration on the day following the lunch at the Algonquin, Kaufman soon informed Dayton that he was going to work with Moss Hart for at least two months. The Kaufman/Hart collaboration on *Merrily We Roll Along* moved ahead rapidly in order to be part of the 1934–35 season. Thus Dayton had to bide her time patiently.

Kaufman was a restless man, who not only paced the floor during work sessions with collaborators, but who also seemed driven to roam mentally from one project to another. Despite the fact that his work habits frequently led to good first acts but disappointing remaining acts, his restlessness or energy propelled him from one collaborator's work space to another. Eventually he returned to Dayton to write *First Lady*, which was scheduled to open in November 1935.

The plot of *First Lady* is constructed around a rivalry between two Washington hostesses: Mrs. Lucy Chase Wayne—the wife of the Secretary of State, and granddaughter of a former President—and Mrs. Irene Hibbard—the wife of a Supreme Court Justice, and the ex-wife of the Prince of Slovania, a country that was absorbed by another after the Great War. Lucy believes that Irene is working to have a young senator become a presidential candidate, and that after the election, Irene will divorce her dull husband to marry the young president, thereby becoming the First Lady. Lucy wishes to thwart Irene's scheme.

Lucy manipulates a women's coalition to support Justice Hibbard, who she thinks is an unlikely candidate for president. Lucy thinks Irene will be tricked into staying with her judicial husband at least until the "boom" fizzles. Unexpectedly, the judge becomes the candidate the party wishes to endorse. Lucy must now use her brains and political savvy to undo this mess she created. She points out to Irene a technicality that proves the ex-princess is not legally divorced from her royal mate. As a result, Irene is forced to convince the judge not to proceed toward the nomination. Secretary of State Wayne becomes the next likely candidate to be endorsed by the party, and Lucy is on her way to becoming the First Lady.

Lucy Chase Wayne was modeled after Katharine Dayton's friend, Alice Roosevelt Longworth, daughter of Theodore Roosevelt. She was married to Nicholas Longworth, who was Speaker of the House, and Mrs. Longworth was a Washington society leader for decades. Jane Cowl played the Lucy Chase Wayne role on Broadway, and she won the approval of the reviewers.

John Anderson's *New York Evening Journal* review applauds the actress: "Miss Cowl plays, and plays with the glint of fine malice, the astute autocrat of the nation's official dinner tables, a political boss in petticoats whose career consists in brewing tempest in her teapots. . . . She (Lucy) is a wonderous character and Miss Cowl plays her superbly."[10] The actress is also given credit with the authors by Brooks Atkinson in the opening paragraph of his *New York Times* review (27 November 1935): "Jane Cowl has conspired with them [the authors] to make a brilliant comedy out of it for the patrons of the Music Box. . . ."

Obviously the production was successful, and the run lasted for 244 performances. The play itself is considered bright, brittle, mischievous, and hilarious with flashes of caustic humor that illuminate the entire political landscape. The humor of the piece continues to entertain more than fifty years after the play's premiere though there have been no recent revivals. *First Lady*—with its leading character a charming, challenging female—is reminiscent of both *Dulcy* and *To the Ladies!*

A film version of *First Lady* was produced by Warner Brothers and released in September 1937. It was not as successful as the play. Some reviewers believed film actress Kay Francis was not as brilliant as Jane Cowl in the role of Lucy.

After *First Lady* opened, Kaufman found he had free time to write. It seemed a propitious time to reactivate his partnership with Edna Ferber. Perhaps Kaufman sensed that Ferber was emotionally and spiritually disturbed and thought work might relieve her depression. Once again on a New Year's Eve, this time as 1935 gave way to 1936, Kaufman and Ferber began earnestly to discuss plot ideas. They began developing a script idea concerned with the hopes, struggles, and ambitions of a group of young theatrical aspirants.

This play, *Stage Door,* is set in the Footlights Club, a residence for young women of the stage. The major plot focuses on idealistic Terry Randall and her two roommates. During act 1 Terry's roommate Louise leaves New York City to return to life in Wisconsin as a married woman. Louise is replaced by Kaye Hamilton, a quiet, hopeful actress who has run away from her sadistic, wealthy husband. Terry's other original roommate is Jean Maitland, who lands a Hollywood contract. Throughout acts 2 and 3 Jean's Hollywood career is charted through letters and news releases. Terry, a talented actress, twice refuses the opportunity to go to Hollywood since she prefers the art of theater.

Terry acquires Jean's cast-off playwright boyfriend Keith Burgess, who writes social protest drama. Terry helps him to flesh out his current play, and the improved script is optioned by a major Broadway producer. Keith's play becomes a commercial success, but his social messages are nearly forgotten when he accepts a contract to write screenplays at a Hollywood studio. Terry is once more alone when a Hollywood executive/agent named David Kingsley invites her to dinner.

Meanwhile, Terry's acting career has been floundering, and eventually she is forced to take a sales position at Macy's department store. As she continues to make the rounds of managers' offices during her lunch hours, other melodramatic events are happening in the lives of her former and present roommates. Louise returns to New York leaving her husband in (Edna Ferber's home state) Wisconsin. Jean visits the Footlights Club since she has come to New York to star in a Broadway production. She donates a large portrait of herself to be hung in the club and leaves the residents atwitter. Kaye commits suicide after she is fired from her role in a play.

Playwright Keith returns from Hollywood for a brief visit and asks Terry to marry him. Terry, no longer enamored of Keith and his new plans, rejects his proposal. It is at this same time that David Kingsley fails to speak of his feelings for Terry; however, he returns within two weeks to prove his devotion. He buys the play that Jean has now abandoned and gives the leading role to Terry, for he is sure she will perform brilliantly.

The authors' role model for Keith Burgess is Clifford Odets, who attracted attention in 1935 with his plays *Waiting for Lefty* and *Awake and Sing*. He was hailed as America's most promising young playwright, but he soon went to Hollywood to write *The General Dies at Dawn,* which was released in 1936. The portrait was so clearly delineated that when reviewer Richard Lockridge referred to the young radical playwright Burgess, he slyly comments: "and no reference, surely, is intended to any living person, ..."[11]

Stage Door opened 22 October 1936, with Margaret Sullavan playing Terry. This play also afforded sixteen other young actresses diverse roles as residents of the club. Ferber, when referring to stagestruck, sincere young women, wrote, "they kill me with their courage and their hope." But she becomes angered in the same paragraph when she recalls that Margaret Sullavan left *Stage Door* in the midst of its success, "throwing about forty people out of work," many of them the type of young people Ferber admired.[12] Sullavan, married to agent Leland Hayward, was pregnant, and her physician advised her to leave the production. She played 169 performances; however, producer Harris decided with the authors not to seek another leading lady. Thus *Stage Door* closed while still doing good business after Sullavan's final performance.

Stage Door was a successful production, and John Mason Brown in his *New York Post* review aptly summarizes the Kaufman/Ferber collaborative efforts: "They supplement each other nicely by combining wit and sentiment so that each comes to the aid of the other. What they see, they may see with different eyes, but they see it clearly and state it in effective stage terms. They both have an adroit and delightful professional touch. And when, as in *Stage Door,* their subject is the theatre, they can be counted upon to do an amusing and interesting job because they are writing about something they both know and love."[13]

In a later paragraph he concisely criticizes the play: "*Stage Door* suffers at present from being too long, from petering out at the end, and from some of its needlessly bitter fist-waving in Hollywood's direction. It is in no sense of the word an important play, but it is an entertaining one. It avoids most of the sentimental pitfalls of its theme; is shrewd and capable as a show; provides an evening of often side-splitting, sometimes touching, and almost always effective theatre."

The film rights for *Stage Door* were sold to RKO-Radio Pictures for $130,000. Morrie Ryskind and Anthony Veiller, hired to write the screenplay, took many liberties with the original script. Katharine Hepburn starred as Terry, and Ginger Rogers costarred in the role of Jean Maitland that had been expanded to fit costar status. The film was a hit, but Kaufman reportedly dismissed it with the comment that it should have been retitled "Screen Door."

A Sketch

Kaufman, at some point during 1936, also wrote a solo sketch titled *Meet the Audience*. This three-character play is set in the sparsely furnished living room of Miss Teitelbaum. She has been acquainted with Mr. Winterbottom for twenty years, and he has just telephoned, asking to see her immediately. Miss Teitelbaum and her maid Lilith both expect Mr. Winterbottom to propose marriage to Miss Teitelbaum. Upon his arrival, he tries to propose something, but is deterred by coughing seizures. The coughing becomes contagious, with Miss Teitelbaum, Lilith, and even the audience joining with Mr. Winterbottom's discomfort. The general coughing throughout the theater makes it impossible to continue the action of the play. Three soldiers beckoned on stage by Teitelbaum and Winterbottom aim their guns at the audience and fire.

This satire on the type of social-protest drama labeled New Realism has several elements similar in effect to a play written in 1936 by Irwin Shaw titled *Bury the Dead*. The Kaufman sketch leads one to believe that audience participation is required. The author indicates in the script, however, that the audiences's coughing is actually coming through the sound system. Shaw used the same device of "spotting" successive speakers to produce the feeling that voices were coming from the house (the audience).

The ending of *Meet the Audience* is both startling and disturbing because it thrusts the audience into the situation. In Shaw's fantasy, which also used a bare stage setting, six corpses, victims of the war, refuse to be buried. At the conclusion, the corpses march off the stage, down the aisles, and out of the theater, thereby becoming a part of the world of the audience.

Kaufman's script seems written for a specific audience—perhaps one of his theater club memberships, which would immediately understand the point of the satire. It is unknown whether *Meet the Audience* was ever produced.

Chapter Five

The Years with Moss Hart

The Trial

Sam H. Harris, the producer, was responsible for introducing George S. Kaufman to young, talented Moss Hart. The latter had written a play titled *Once in a Lifetime* that interested Harris, but he realized the script needed considerable polishing and rewriting. The story was timely and engaging since it centered on a three-person vaudeville team who decide to go to Hollywood to seek fame and fortune in the burgeoning talking-picture industry.

Harris agreed to produce the play if Kaufman would collaborate with Hart on the script revisions. Hart eagerly accepted the condition. He was an avid admirer of the comedies written by Kaufman and Connelly. When Hart started writing comedies rather than serious plays, he patterned his work after the successful duo's endeavors. Eventually Kaufman decided to take on the project, and this marked the first time he collaborated with a total stranger on a major project.

In December 1929 the two playwrights began their daily meetings in an attempt to reshape *Once in a Lifetime.* In "Men at Work"—an introduction written for a volume of six plays by Kaufman and Hart published in 1942—Hart recalls that "our working day consisted of ten o'clock in the morning until exhausted—somewhere, perhaps, around one or two o'clock the next morning—with perhaps fifteen minutes out for such meals as Mr. Kaufman considered necessary to keep alive."[1] This routine, or a variation of it, was maintained over a period of ten months until the play's Broadway opening on 24 September 1930.

It was this experience that taught Moss Hart the meaning of the timeworn phrase, "Plays are not written, but rewritten." The first revised script proved not to please the out-of-town tryout audiences. After struggling through mid-May performances in Atlantic City and Brighton Beach, a small Brooklyn community close to Coney Island, Kaufman informed Hart that he could contribute nothing more to the script. Hart realized this would be the end of his opportunity unless he developed a new approach that would strengthen the disappointing second and third acts. Hart also knew his ideas must appeal to Kaufman immediately and induce the senior playwright to remain on the project.

Hart's determination and previous theater experience assisted him as he invented a new outline for the weak acts. Within twenty-four hours he had a new scenario that he memorized in order to present his ideas effectively to Kaufman. The following morning Hart set out to woo Kaufman back to the play. After Hart's hour-long recitation, Kaufman invited the junior playwright to move into his home for the summer so the two could work continuously on the script.

The new version of the play opened in Philadelphia the first of September. The revised second act was an immediate success, but there were still problems in the third. Comments made by Sam Harris to Hart suddenly illuminated the reason for the troublesome third act: "Once this show gets underway nobody ever talks to each other. They just keep pounding away like hell and running in and out of that scenery. It's a noisy play, kid, you take my word for it."[2]

A newly inspired Moss Hart immediately rearranged the third act. With only three performances left in the Philadelphia run, he convinced Kaufman to try the new version on stage. The quiet scene in the third act worked perfectly; Kaufman and Hart left Philadelphia with a script destined to be a box office hit.

The plot revolves around the antics of three performers who were an unsuccessful vaudeville team: George Lewis, the dullest but luckiest member of the team; May Daniels, who possesses a quick mind and a hearty sense of humor; and Jerry Hyland, a talented salesman/schemer. Since they have no bookings lined up, they decide to leave vaudeville, which is dying, and become part of the booming talking-picture business located in Hollywood. In act 1, scene 2, while the trio is traveling west on a train, May recognizes Helen Hobart, a former vaudeville trouper who has become America's foremost movie critic. May visits with Helen, who quickly becomes enthusiastic about the idea of an elocution school for Hollywood silent film stars. May tells Helen that Jerry, George, and herself are a voice culture team that has been working in England. After the act 1, scene 3 arrival in Hollywood, Helen arranges a meeting for the team with Herman Glogauer, a film studio owner. Glogauer buys the idea and decides to support the voice school in his studio.

The school is in operation as act 2 begins, but it is soon learned that the voice educational program will be instantly abolished. All appears lost for the vaudeville trio until George seizes the opportunity to speak to Glogauer, who is impressed with George's courage to speak the truth. Actually the truth is the opinion of New York playwright Lawrence Vail, who was brought to Hollywood and forgotten by the studio. George is rehired by Glogauer and put in charge of a new production that will star his girl friend, Susan Walker, whom he met on the train coming west. George hires May and Jerry to assist him in his new position.

Act 3, scene 1 is a satirical glimpse at the final day of shooting a film. Glogauer visits the set to congratulate George for completing the picture on schedule and to present George with a token of his esteem— a one-hundred-and-six-piece gold dinner set with George's initials set in diamonds. Following the presentation, however, Glogauer discovers the wrong scenario was used to make the picture. Glogauer immediately fires George and his assistants. Act 3, scene 2 finds May returning by train to the East Coast. She learns that the picture has been released, and that it was an instant success. George, who has been reinstated at Glogauer's studio, summons May to return.

The last scene of the play takes place at the studio where George has once more done something stupid that will eventually become praiseworthy—he purchased two thousand aeroplanes in order to get one free. Glogauer is not upset since the other studios believe he is starting a new trend in making aeroplane pictures, and they want to purchase his planes. The story ends with the studio being demolished, which Glogauer believes is another new trend set by his Golden Boy George.

Kaufman made his Broadway acting debut in the role of playwright Lawrence Vail. Kaufman took pleasure in the role because his character has several opportunities to berate the film industry.

> *VAIL:* (Act 2, addressing George) Dr. Lewis, I think Hollywood and this daring industry of yours is the most God-awful thing I've ever run into. Everybody behaving in the most fantastic fashion—nobody acting like a human being. I'm brought out here, like a hundred others, paid a fat salary—nobody notices me. Not that I might be any good—it's just an indication. Thousands of dollars thrown away every day.

Although neither Kaufman nor Hart had visited Hollywood, they learned about working in a studio from friends and from stories printed in *Variety*, the journal of show business. Kaufman had refused numerous offers to write for Hollywood studios. He preferred to observe from the East Coast and to comment rather than join the fray. Playing the role of Vail provided Kaufman with the opportunity to personally express his vision of life in a Hollywood studio.

Kaufman's performance was a novelty that appealed to audiences. Brooks Atkinson, who would become the dean of reviewers serving thirty-one years in the same post, comments in his *New York Times* review (25, September 1930) that "Mr. Kaufman, who was doubtless unnerved last evening by the long salute of applause that greeted his appearance, had little fantasy to give them. By the time of his second appearance in the last act he had recovered." Obviously Kaufman's acting ability was less significant than his talent as a playwright or director. Yet he remained in the Vail role until April 1931, when he needed to concentrate on other projects, including a revue with Howard Dietz titled "The Band Wagon."

Hart also took his turn as an actor in the Lawrence Vail role. He opened in the California production of *Once in a Lifetime* and later played Vail in New York. However, Hart proved to be an uninspired actor. The acting experience allowed him to sample the delights of his newfound fame. But fortune was also part of his success especially since Kaufman gave Hart sixty percent of the royalities. The income from the play was steady despite the worsening economic situation gripping the country. *Once in a Lifetime* was the type of entertainment that appealed to audiences who wanted to forget their cares of the day. The productions in New York and Hollywood were playing to nearly full houses; the Broadway run of the show was 401 performances. The film rights were sold to Universal Pictures, and a successful movie was released by 1932.

While there is little that is theatrically inventive in *Once in a Lifetime,* its viewpoint is fresh and humorous. Eleanor Flexner, a critic who is not a Kaufman enthusiast, comments that Kaufman and Hart "have certainly concocted between them one of the most excruciatingly funny plays of our day." She continues her praise with, "What raises it high above the level of casual folly is the idea around which the play centers. They have not only burlesqued the insanity which is the byword of Hollywood, but have focused that insanity at a particular moment which furnishes them with an inherently dramatic situation: the advent of the 'talkies.'"[3] The play continues to be enjoyable and it has frequently been restaged by notable theater companies such as Arena Stage in Washington, D.C., Circle in the Square (New York), Royal

Shakespeare Company (London, 1980), and Mark Taper Theatre (Los Angeles).

The Kaufman and Hart collaboration generated a play that is remarkably without any distinguishing individual flourishes. Yet the blending of wit, intelligence, phraseology, and theatrical flair is seamless. During a brief curtain call speech on opening night, Kaufman attributed eighty percent of the play to Moss Hart,[4] but many reviewers were so sure that the highly charged comic lines were Kaufman's that several of them ignored Hart while others barely alluded to him.

Prior to the Broadway opening of *Once in a Lifetime,* Kaufman had indicated to Hart an interest in collaborating on another project even though he did not have anything specific in mind. Following the successful opening, Hart had a number of other interesting offers that he pursued over the next few years. Within a relatively short time Hart came into his own. However, before the end of the decade, Hart's name would become permanently linked with Kaufman's.

Another Round

Early in 1934 Hart contacted Kaufman with an outline for a new play, *Merrily We Roll Along,* which departed from the traditional manner of presenting time on stage. Instead of developing a plot from the beginning to the end, Hart desired to commence at the conclusion of the plot and have each scene move backwards in time: act 1, scene 1 is set in 1934, and act 3, scene 3 (the last scene) takes place in 1916. The play presents the life-style and success attained by the protagonist Richard Niles in the first act, then it dissects character motivations and relationships, showing how each situation evolved toward its final outcome. It is an interesting technique, but frequently proves unsettling to audiences until the pattern of events is made clear. Harold Pinter, the noted British avant-garde playwright, used this same technique in his script *Betrayal* written in 1978.

The intervening years since *Once in a Lifetime* had allowed Hart to become established as a theatrical talent; he had created two hits—*Face the Music* (directed by Kaufman) and *As Thousands Cheer.* He proved to be not only talented, but also as prolific and untiring as Kaufman. The two men were anxious to commence their work on *Merrily We Roll Along,* which is a play of epic proportions. The final script requires ninety-one actors, one hundred and fifty costumes, nine scenes with nine different settings, and two stage managers to handle all the details. It became the most expensive nonmusical play ever to be presented in Harris's Music Box Theatre where it played for 155 performances.

Richard Niles, a successful Broadway playwright, and his wife Althea Royce, an actress who seems a bit past her prime, are entertaining their friends following the opening of Richard's current play. The reviews arrive and the production is proclaimed a hit. Althea in a moment of jealousy and bitterness throws iodine in the eyes of the leading lady of Richard's new play. Following this scene, the plot moves backwards in time to examine the turning points in Richard's life. The story reveals how Richard and Althea—as well as some of the other characters—reached the moments in their lives when their successes and failures are established. The plot examines both Richard's relationship to Julia Glenn and to Jonathan Crale. It shows how Richard and Althea met and how their relationship evolved into marriage; how Richard's life with his first wife Helen ended in divorce; and how several characters during the intervening years experience career shifts.

The play has an antimaterialistic theme that was popular during the 1934–35 season. It is the most serious play written by these two writers up to this time; and, as a result of this excursion into less comedic drama, the critics began to tear its intent apart. Both Elanor Flexner and John Howard Lawson are convinced that the backward action is satisfactory but that the play is "inherently false and superficial" because of the authors' point of view. Kaufman and Hart are accused of evading real character analysis and conflict development by substituting effective curtain incidents at the conclusion of scenes—Althea throwing the iodine at actress Ivy Carroll, Niles's attack on his friend Crale, Althea's claim on Richard in front of Helen. These dramatic events result in irony and theatricality that Flexner and Lawson label as either surprise or superficial melodrama.[5]

From a present-day perspective, when epic theater has come into its own and not every play has to be steeped in character analysis to be considered important, *Merrily We Roll Along* may be evaluated with a different criterion. While this play does not truly emulate the theater of German director Erwin Piscator (1893–1966), who evolved the first epic play in 1927, *Merrily We Roll Along* uses Piscator's basic formula that requires a range of events occurring in a number of different places over a lengthy stretch of time. Also Piscator was extremely theatrical in the staging of his epic play. He utilized projections, treadmills, and all types of devices to adapt the action to the stage. He desired to comment upon society and to arouse the critical faculties of his audience. This seems similar to the intent of Kaufman and Hart although they did not focus on stage machinery and devices, but instead used irony and theatricality. They designed the play to draw its effects from displays of production richness and theatrical treatment. For example, act 2, scene 3 is written with numerous stage directions precisely set to achieve the maximum theatrical effectiveness in the scene: "Again she [Althea] clutches him by the hand and hauls him across the room. This time a sudden movement of the crowd keeps Helen from following, and in a twinkling there is a solid mass of people between her and Richard."

It is not important whether Niles has major talent that was wasted. The key seems to be that here is a man who lost his idealism about art and life, replacing it with the material tokens of success. The play is a comment upon society and its pressures upon individuals, particularly artists, rather than an in-depth study of a specific man. It is epic rather than realistic.

There is another element in this play that engaged reviewers and critics. They were constantly trying to match several onstage characters with real people. There was speculation concerning the character Sam Frankel, a brash composer. He was assumed to be a takeoff of George Gershwin, while the sharp-spoken writer Julia Glenn characterized Dorothy Parker. Kaufman admitted to "traces" of Parker, who was not one of his favorite persons, in the Glenn characterization.[6] A minor character, Val Burnett, evokes memories of crooner Rudy Vallee who became famous in 1928 by singing into a megaphone.

After closing on Broadway, *Merrily We Roll Along* opened in Philadelphia for a two-week stint. The original production had recovered its layout costs despite the expensive sets, costumes, and numerous salaries. Metro-Goldwyn-Mayer purchased the film rights but never produced it. And *Merrily We Roll Along* served as the inspiration for a musical play created by Stephen Sondheim in 1981. Although the musical with the same title as the play was not a success on Broadway, it has had several independent productions over the past five years.

A Blockbuster

During the spring of 1934 George S. Kaufman made his first trip to California in order to work with Hart on *Merrily We Roll Along*. It was at this time that Hart conceived the idea of a play based on an eccentric family who lives in total freedom, indulging in unrestricted activities that pose no threats to anyone. While they both liked the idea, Kaufman and Hart were too busy to begin developing it. Each had separate projects and plans that kept them from working together: First Kaufman was involved with "Bring On the Girls" followed by his writing of the screenplay *A Night at the Opera*. Meanwhile Hart went on a five-and-a-half-month cruise around the world during which he worked on the new musical *Jubilee*, a project that kept him occupied after his return. Then Kaufman was busy with *First Lady* followed by *Stage Door*. Finally, in the summer of 1936 they scheduled time to collaborate in California on their third venture.

Kaufman and Hart commenced discussing a project, then after several days of contemplation it was discarded. It was then that Kaufman reminded Hart of his earlier idea about the slightly mad family in which each member does precisely what he or she desires without the rest of the family interfering. The playwrights completed the draft in five weeks and spent two weeks polishing the lines, but months passed as they tried to title the play before its Broadway opening on 14 December 1936.

Kaufman and Hart developed a pattern for working during their collaborations. They liked to discuss an idea casually, sometimes letting it incubate in their minds for a period of time before scheduling regular work sessions. Kaufman and Hart then set up a daily schedule in a location where they could be free of interruption. The playwrights talked for several weeks, enlarging and clarifying the idea. Once both of them were thinking systematically, they started putting the ideas in writing. With this approach, they created *You Can't Take It with You*.

The action of the play is set in the New York home of Grandpa Martin Vanderhof. His daughter Penelope Sycamore, her husband Paul, their daughters Alice and Essie, plus Essie's husband Ed Carmichael share grandpa's home. Other members of this freewheeling household include two black household servants and a lodger named Mr. De Pinna. There is also an interesting assortment of visitors to the Sycamore home: ballet teacher Boris Kolenkhov, the Grand Duchess Olga Katrina, actress Gay Wellington, and governmental agents from the IRS and FBI.

The only member of the Sycamore family to maintain a regular job in the everyday world is Alice, the elder daughter. She is in love with her boss's son, Tony Kirby, who loves her in return. The romantic subplot intermingles gaily with the family's confrontations with agents

from the FBI and IRS, who come to the house to investigate two separate activities: Grandpa never pays his income taxes, and Ed prints
slogans that have roused the interest of the FBI, seekers of anarchists
and other criminals.

In act 2 every situation becomes complicated. Tony Kirby brings his
parents to meet the Sycamores on the evening prior to the date arranged for their visit. His stuffy, conventional parents are disgusted by
the family of nonconformists and their friends. Alice is upset with
Tony—because he brought his parents on the wrong evening—and
with her family because they are not like other people. The evening
concludes when the FBI agents search the premises and discover that
firecrackers are being made in the cellar of the Sycamores' house. Their
raid results in an explosion at the end of act 2 that is a befitting climax
to the antics of nearly everyone involved in the plot: the FBI agents
trundle everyone off to jail.

The following morning brings solutions to the chaos. The Alice/
Tony romance is righted before the final curtain, and the problems
with the IRS and FBI are solved. Tony's father visits the Sycamore
home once again: he succumbs to the idea of living by impulse and the
theory that "life is simple and kind of beautiful if you let it come to
you."

This play has been lauded by nearly every reviewer and critic, with
few exceptions. Eleanor Flexner does manage to snipe at the play la-
beling the plot "hackneyed," the situations "threadbare," and the love
scenes "long and trite."[7] In spite of the objections, *You Can't Take It
with You* became an American classic. With the original run of 837
performances it became the fifth longest run in the history of Broadway; its film sale to Columbia Pictures was for the record-setting
amount of two hundred thousand dollars; the 1938 film was awarded
the Academy Award for Best Picture; the play received the Pulitzer
Prize for drama in 1937; and it continues to remain popular beyond
its fiftieth year. Many productions are mounted annually by university
and community theaters. In 1965 and again in 1983 Ellis Rabb staged
professional revivals of the play. The latter production had a successful
Broadway run with a stellar cast headed by Jason Robards. The play
also continues to intrigue Europeans, and productions have been staged
in major continental cities within the past ten years.

Brooks Atkinson in his *New York Times* review (15 December 1936)
comments on the style of comedy in *You Can't Take It with You* and
tells how it differs from *Once in a Lifetime,* which "mowed the audience

down under a machine-gun of low comedy satire." *You Can't Take It with You* does not seem to be overloaded with wisecracks but rather it appears to be a "more spontaneous piece of hilarity" written with "a dash of affection to season the humor." The authors have "a knack for extravagances of word and episode and an eye for hilarious incongruities."

Six years later Atkinson further explains the Kaufman/Hart style: "The plots serve as frames for the fireworks; the romantic scenes are dutiful gestures towards the conventions of the stage. But the flurry of gags, the bitterness and speed of the attacks upon stupidity, the loudness of the humor, the precision of the phrasing are remarkable in the field of popular comedy."[8]

The objections to *You Can't Take It with You* seem to arise from the lack of any directly stated philosophy. Some critics ignored the clear image of the American spirit of tolerance and happiness that is derived from the benefits of democracy. This was an especially important message given the world situation in 1936, when the freedom of individuals was being trampled under Hitler's boots. Rather these critics carp about the fact that Kaufman "has remained essentially the columnist he was during his early newspaper career—one, that is to say, whose chief business it is to make random comments upon a thousand things. Members of that profession are not required to develop a philosophy or to have anything independent to say."[9]

The critical commentary about the lack of philosophy, while a somewhat popular issue in the late 1930s, has had little bearing on the life of *You Can't Take It with You*. The play continues to thrive due to its indelible spirit, its clearly delineated humor, and its fascinating, lovable characters. It is, according to Atkinson's assessment in his newspaper review, "Funny without being shrill, sensible without being earnest." Certainly this comedy is one of the gems of American drama.

A Musical

After the success of *You Can't Take It with You* Kaufman and Hart wanted, as soon as possible, to begin another project. They shrewdly decided to undertake a different type of venture rather than another comedy that surely would be compared to their blockbuster. Thus they determined that a musical would be the appropriate vehicle. Both writers were pleased with their decision, especially since they had never pooled their experience and talent in such an endeavor.

Kaufman and Hart decided that the score for their new project should be provided by Ira and George Gershwin. The story line of the book was to revolve around the making of a musical. The plans for creating this work never fell into place, however, so it was dropped by spring, 1937. The idea was never resurrected due, in part, to a devastating loss that occurred on 11 July 1937, when George Gershwin, at age thirty-nine, died unexpectedly of a brain tumor.

Another plot scheme for a musical was abandoned before Kaufman and Hart settled on a satirical musical featuring the character of the then president of the United States—Franklin D. Roosevelt, who was serving his second term. This novel concept had a few minor precedents—a sketch written for *Garrick Gaieties* in 1925 had as the principal character Calvin Coolidge, and another sketch from Moss Hart's *As Thousands Cheer* showcased a Herbert Hoover character. Kaufman and Hart were certain that an entire musical with President Roosevelt as a principal character would cause a sensation.

The famous songwriters Richard Rogers and Lorenz Hart (not related to Moss), who had been a successful team since their first success in 1920 titled *Poor Little Rich Girl,* agreed to create the score. The musical's title *I'd Rather Be Right,* was suggested by Roger's wife, Dorothy. It is from a popular saying attributed to Henry Clay, the American statesman who served as Secretary of State from 1825 to 1829. His phrase often quoted in the 1930s was "I'd rather be right than President." *I'd Rather Be Right,* produced by Sam Harris, was scheduled for rehearsals in September and a two-week tryout-run in Boston early in October 1937.

The Fourth of July celebrations in New York's Central Park provide the setting for *I'd Rather Be Right,* labeled a Musical Revue by the playwrights. A young couple, Phil and Peggy, arrive in the park early in the evening in order to hear the holiday concert. They are discouraged about their future together since their hope to marry is connected to Phil's promotion at work. He has just learned that his boss, Mr. Maxwell, has canceled his plans to open a new office where Phil's new job was to be located. Mr. Maxwell chose to dismiss his business expansion plans since the Depression has not abated, and uncertainty about President Roosevelt's fiscal planning is widespread. It becomes necessary for the president to balance the nation's budget before Maxwell will consider expansion.

As Phil and Peggy listen to the music playing in the distance, they are approached by a figure who turns out to be the president. Roosevelt finds the couple pleasing, and he decides to try to balance the budget so they can marry. Unfortunately the Cabinet, Supreme Court, and other consultants create enough objections to all the president's ideas that the problem remains despite his valiant efforts. Eventually the president, during his holiday "fireside chat" held in the park, advises the citizenry to take heart. He suggests to Phil that he should proceed with his plans to marry Peggy despite the budget dilemma. It is at this point that Phil wakes up to discover the president's attention to his personal problems has been a dream. However, Phil remains persuaded to marry Peggy immediately rather than wait for the national economy to be strengthened.

Kaufman and Hart, while writing the book, decided the best performer to create F.D.R. on stage was George M. Cohan, known affectionately as the "Yankee-Doodle Dandy." Cohan had not starred in a musical on Broadway since 1927, when he appeared in *The Merry Malones,* for which he had created the book and score by himself. His return to the stage starring as F.D.R. in *I'd Rather Be Right* drew numerous rave reviews, and he received thunderous acclaim from audiences.

The plot of the musical was considered to be daring because it depicted the incumbent head of state. The collective opinion of the press was that the barbed wit and sharp jests made at the expense of President Roosevelt, his Cabinet, the Supreme Court, and other governmental entities could only be tolerated in the United States. This was an important consideration since the threat of war and the stories of tyrannical abuse in Europe were growing daily. This musical reminded Americans of the virtues of the democratic way of life.

While *I'd Rather Be Right* is political satire, it is somewhat playful, and opinions are obviously in favor of Roosevelt. It is not as biting as Kaufman's earlier 1930s political musicals—*Of Thee I Sing* and *Let 'Em Eat Cake.* However, several other political characters are not treated as gently as is the president.

The New Deal generally is under attack, and especially the tax programs. Mr. Maxwell becomes a balloon salesman in Central Park, where he explains to President Roosevelt that numerous taxes are consuming his profits and causing his business to falter. As he cites each tax, he pops a balloon—effectively impressing upon the audience that his popped balloons represent thirty separate taxes.

This is still a gentle rebuff compared to the treatment received by the Supreme Court justices: The "nine old men" are burlesqued unmercifully. The members of the Cabinet also take their lashes on stage, with Postmaster General James Farley carrying the brunt of the satire. He has lines that make him a villain to every tax-paying American: "Hot dog! New taxes, boys! Wheee!" These people are obstructers who represent stupidity and bureaucracy. They surround the president while he remains a sensitive, affable father figure, but his policies and projects remain fair game.

Even his Federal Theatre Project, a 1935–1939 nationwide network designed to provide employment to needy professional theater people in socially useful jobs, receives a few critical volleys from Kaufman and Hart. They are particularly critical of the amount of money the project spends on productions. In *I'd Rather Be Right* Kaufman and Hart, who always recognized exciting theatrical practices, incorporated techniques developed by the Living Newspaper Unit, which presented plays to educate the public about social issues of the day. The balloon scene is a takeoff on one of the unit's techniques. Other audience-educating methods employed by the unit included the use of projections and other visual, innovative teaching tricks that capture the attention of the viewers, who were usually nontraditional theatergoers.

I'd Rather Be Right ran for 289 performances followed by a tour. It was another successful venture by Kaufman and Hart whose names were beginning to be bonded permanently in the minds of theater enthusiasts.

A Salute to the Theater

In the spring of 1938, when Kaufman was experimenting with radio appearances as a guest panelist on *Information Please,* he and Hart began toying with new ideas for their next script. Hart was keen on creating a cavalcade drama. Originally Hart thought about an American cavalcade, but British playwright Noel Coward had scooped Hart when his 1931 English patriotic spectacle titled *Cavalcade* was staged. Theatrical cavalcades created in England and the United States share some of the presentational ideas and techniques that Piscator experimented with and his follower Bertold Brecht perfected.

Hart remained fascinated by the cavalcade idea and proposed to Kaufman that they write a cavalcade about theater. Eventually this concept evolved into a play that not only traces the history of Broadway theater from 1900, but also parades scenes from the best-remembered plays and incorporates their poster art. The production, called *The*

Fabulous Invalid, became a gallery of snapshots from the American theater's hall of fame.

The Fabulous Invalid is the ever-dying, but never dead art of theater. The title also refers to a specific theater that begins its history in glamorous style but sinks to a tawdry existence after the 1929 stock market crash. The play opens on a gala evening in 1900, when the Alexandria Theatre is presenting its first offering to the public. The play and the theater are both successfully received by a glittering audience of socialites. Following the performance, leading lady Paula Kingsley collapses and dies. Her husband and leading man Laurence Brooks kills himself, for he can not bear life without her. Since there is a special dispensation for actors who die in the theater, the ghosts of these two actors have the choice of either going to heaven or "hanging around" the theater until it no longer exists. Paula and Larry select staying in the theater. Over the intervening years they watch the Alexandria's owner, John Carleton, struggle to maintain his theater during various crises. The ghosts also witness the triumphs on stage. Everything is going well until the sudden crash of the stock market, when Carleton loses everything including the Alexandria.

The theater is converted in 1930 into a movie house for talking pictures. But the movie people also have a difficult time making their expenses during the Depression years; finally they too are forced to close their Alexandria enterprise. When the theater is placed on auction, Carleton tries to buy it back. He is outbid by an unidentified person, who turns the Alexandria into a burlesque house. This operation is moderately successful, but it succumbs to one raid too many.

The theater stands empty and there is no hope of securing a new owner. Paula and Larry are told by the character named The Man From Up There that they must go to heaven. The final degradation of the Alexandria is when the lobby entrance is boarded up, and the theater stands forlorn, proclaiming it is an abandoned building. All seems lost forever as Paula and Larry begin to take leave of their beloved theater. Suddenly a group of young players tear down the boarded entrance and come into the theater. They are led by an enthusiastic, talented youth, who plans to restore the art of theater to the stage of the Alexandria. Thus Paula and Larry can remain in their beloved theater since it will survive.

The Fabulous Invalid shows Kaufman and Hart's devotion to the theater. However, the depth of their affection seems to overwhelm them, resulting in their inability to make the play more than a spectacular tribute. It continually falls short of its mark due to superficiality. The playwrights attempt to define the necessity of theater in everyone's life by saying that theater lifts "men's spirits above the reality of their lives" and "theatre can bring beauty and magic and wonder into your lives." The play is obviously sentimental in tone, which is uncharacteristic of Kaufman and Hart, and it fails to rouse the appropriate sense of the pride, talent, and spirit that brought American theater to international prominence within the span of history it portrays.

Once again the playwriting team borrowed techniques from the Federal Theatre's Living Newspaper Unit. One example is their reliance upon the Alexandria Theatre as the script's major character, which was undoubtedly inspired by similar usage of a tenement building in a production mounted by the unit. Another method that they adopted was the utilization of the "everyman" figure—Paula and Larry—whose questions create opportunities for educating the audience. Also just as the Living Newspaper frequently used displays of historical illustrations, Kaufman and Hart exhibited show posters throughout *The Fabulous Invalid*. These techniques were also similar to those used in the plays of German playwright/director Bertolt Brecht, who had worked with Piscator. Brecht was experimenting with these techniques in Europe under the banner of Epic Theatre methods. These theatrical conventions would become more commonly used after World War II, but Kaufman and Hart, recognizing their value, unabashedly introduced them into the commercial theatre, which was usually the bastion of conservative practices.

The play is trendy in other respects. Characters who return to the stage after death as ghosts, without any horrific connotations, were popular in the 1930s and 1940s. Many plays, including the classic *Blithe Spirit* (1941) by Noel Coward, fit into this genre.

In *The Fabulous Invalid* Kaufman and Hart also gave their public approval to such socially conscious theater groups as the new Mercury Theatre, whose leader was Orson Welles, for the playwrights tailored the saviors of the Alexandria Theatre to fit the pattern of Welles and his company. Malcolm Goldstein mentions that Kaufman had been interested in this particular group since its first production opened in the fall of 1937.[10]

The Fabulous Invalid was not a critical success and its run lasted only sixty-five performances. But it is a work filled with richly detailed information about theater in America and our cultural heritage during the first thirty-eight years of the twentieth century. The script's ongoing value is its invaluable illustrations of many 1930s theatrical techniques as well as its nostalgic glimpse at American theater.

Actually Kaufman and Hart had been involved with another project that preceded *The Fabulous Invalid* to Broadway. This was a topical revue with Max Gordon as producer. Kaufman and Hart frequently assisted Gordon's productions by financially supporting the production, by giving advice during rehearsals, and by doctoring when necessary. For this revue titled "Sing Out the News," Kaufman and Hart were credited as associate producers. This was first time they were titled producers, but both would continue to serve in this capacity throughout the rest of their careers.

During the summer of 1938, when Hitler annexed Austria and began to focus on Czechoslovakia, "Sing Out the News" became the producers' opportunity to defend the American liberal tradition through dance, song, and sketch. The two playwrights wrote some of the sketches, but they mainly reworked those written by Charles Friedman, who had been hired by Gordon to write the show.

One of the surviving sketches credited to Kaufman and Hart is "Gone with the Revolution." The plot depicts a script conference at Metro-Goldwyn-Mayer studio called during the filming of an extravaganza about Marie Antoinette. The problem is that the story demands a revolution, and the Hays Code (Hollywood's strict self-regulatory charter of do's and don'ts) would never allow it. Each star also objects to being in a film that has a revolution as part of the action, but the problem is resolved by staging a token revolution acted by four extras.

After the opening on 24 September 1938, the show ran for only 105 performances. Hart, Kaufman, and Gordon—the sole backers—lost the cost of mounting the production. Yet Kaufman and Hart were undoubtedly too immersed in staging *The American Way* to fret.

A Patriotic Stance

The second Kaufman and Hart production of the 1938–39 theater season was another spectacular epic. Hart's desire to write an American cavalcade persisted especially since the darkening war clouds over Western Europe seemed to dictate the need for a lecture on Americanization, a treatise on tradition, and a call to nationalism. This was the intent for *The American Way*. Other playwrights felt the same need to write plays with patriotic themes for that season, including Robert E.

Sherwood, the winner of the Pulitzer Prize for his *Abe Lincoln in Illinois*.

Kaufman and Hart created a twenty-scene chronicle of the life of the nation from 1896 to 1936 as seen through the eyes of a German immigrant, who loved America because it stood for freedom. Martin Gunther, a cabinetmaker, settled in Mapleton, Ohio. When the play begins in 1896, he is meeting his wife and two small children, who have just arrived in the United States. It is with bursting pride that Martin introduces his family to Mapleton and the American way of life that is based on freedom. In a later scene Martin's talent and belief in democracy bring him to the attention of the town banker, Samuel Brockton, who helps Martin establish a furniture factory. The venture prospers, and the family becomes Americanized. But then the declaration of American involvement in World War I forces the Gunthers to make agonizing choices of loyalty to their adopted land. Martin supports his son's decision to enlist in the American army, and the family suffers the loss of their only son, who perishes on a European battlefield.

Prosperity and assimilation continue for the Gunthers throughout the 1920s, but in 1929 Martin loses his factory as a result of trying to stop a run on Brockton's bank. Despite this newest adversity, Martin continues to keep his faith in freedom. The 1930s introduce new problems, and eventually an uneasiness spreads across the land: there are persons in America who advance the cause and philosophy of Hitler, the latest European tyrant.

On the night of Martin and Irma's fiftieth wedding anniversary in 1936, he is beaten to death by brown-uniformed Bundists as he implores his grandson and other inductees not to join the organization. Martin is victorious in death over the fanaticism of the group, for his grandson returns to the American way of thinking. Martin is given the funeral of a civic hero/leader, and he is eulogized as a true American.

A simple plot outline of this obviously sentimental play does not begin to give a sense of the pageantry involved in the production. John Mason Brown summarizes the effect of the whole in his *New York Post* review (23 January 1934): "As a drama it may be no more than an awfully well managed parade, staged in honor of a cause which has always had your enthusiastic belief. Yet as a parade it does its eye-filling and memory-stirring job extraordinarily well." *The American Way* was a decidedly impressive spectacle created to fill the vast Center Theatre in Rockefeller Center, which seated more than thirty-eight hundred persons. This space had never been used before to house a nonmusical production.

Crowds of actors were needed for the mass town scenes set for community picnics, election campaign meetings, armistice celebration, run on the bank, and country club dance. They filled the cavernous stage replete with revolving stages and usable side stages. The action never stopped, but flashed from one acting area to another. The reviewers praised the spectacle, the staging, and the message.

The production was the most expensive of the 1938-39 season and required the support of two producers—Sam Harris and Max Gordon. One of the reasons so much money was lavished on this production was due to the influx of visitors anticipated for the New York World's Fair scheduled to open on 30 April 1939. It was believed the huge theater would be filled by tourists during the summer months, but the fair did not create the expected demand for tickets, so the production closed for a short vacation after 164 performances. After a one-month hiatus, it reopened and ran an additional eighty performances which was not a bad record considering the size of the theater.

The American Way in its published edition is dedicated to Beatrice; this is the only time Kaufman dedicated a play to his wife. Kaufman in his fiftieth year had taken more of an interest in the social life Beatrice conducted. While their circle of friends still consisted of Woollcott and other Algonquin members, they were also part of the world of journalism and politics with W. Averell Harriman, Ralph Pulitzer, Herbert Bayard Swope, and others. In their company Kaufman heard the latest turns in national and international events, so this was a time when he was more in touch with the world beyond his own.

The Return to Comedy

A promise made to ebullient Alexander Woollcott resulted in the next Kaufman and Hart comedy, *The Man Who Came to Dinner*. In 1938 Woollcott had asked his two friends to consider writing a play in which he could act. More than a year passed before they began work on this vehicle for Woollcott, but by summer of 1939 they completed a draft of the script for and about Woollcott. Kaufman's long-standing friendship of twenty-five years with this leader of the Algonquin Wits afforded him the knowledge of the many-sided Woollcott personality, and Hart's friendship with Woollcott was of a thirteen-year duration.

Together they fashioned a stage version of the "fabulous monster" that even the subject loved.

Alexander Woollcott—author, critic, renowned wit, radio artist, lover of murder mysteries, and raconteur—was one of America's most widely known personages in the twenties and thirties. His personality became a legend in his own time. He was a welcome guest at most fashionable abodes in the United States, including 1600 Pennsylvania Avenue.

Woollcott's stage persona in *The Man Who Came to Dinner* is named Sheridan Whiteside, who is a famous speaker and radio personality. He is on a speaking tour and becomes the unwilling dinner guest of Mr. and Mrs. Stanley in their home in a small Ohio town. Upon Whiteside's departure from the Stanleys', he slips on the ice and breaks his hip. He is confined to the Stanleys' home during his six-week convalescence. He despotically takes over the house and runs it as his own: his friends visit from points east and west, his radio program is aired from the Stanleys' home, and his intrigues reach out from his lair in Ohio to entrap the unsuspecting. The romance of Maggie Cutler, secretary to Whiteside, and Bert Jefferson, a local newspaper man, is one of the major strands of the plot that Whiteside tries to undermine. Just when Whiteside has done as much damage as possible to the Stanley family and Maggie, he is ready to return to the world beyond the Stanleys' home. As he is leaving the premises, he falls on the ice again and is returned to the Stanleys' home, apparently having suffered another broken hip.

Several of Woollcott's friends were also depicted in the comedy: the character named Banjo represented comedian Harpo Marx; the naturalist Metz was based on Dr. Gustav Eckstein, a professor at the University of Cincinnati; seductive actress Lorraine Sheldon was a caricature of stage star Gertrude Lawrence; and the egocentric composer/playwright Beverly Carlton was a takeoff of suave Noel Coward. The real names of more than forty famous people who numbered among Woollcott's friends were mentioned—Walt Disney, H. G. Wells, Lady Astor, Shirley Temple, Somerset Maugham, Hattie Carnegie, and Cary Grant show the variety of friends.

The play was an instant success. The theater was ready for a rollicking comedy. Atkinson (*New York Times,* 17 October 1939) states "Mr. Hart and Mr. Kaufman have put together a fantastic piece of nonsense, with enough plot to serve and a succession of witty rejoinders to keep it hilarious." Burns Mantle (*New York Daily News,* 17 October 1939) claims the play drew laughter "from normally happy playgoers who like their fun touched with a certain sophistication and edged with those boldnesses in speech that startle without offense." This play provided a respite from the political tensions of a world on the brink of another world war. It was the "hottest ticket" in town during the 1939–40 season, which is even more impressive when considering several of the major plays of the year: *The Philadelphia Story* starring Katharine Hepburn: *Key Largo* with Paul Muni; *The Boys from Syracuse*; *The Corn Is Green*; and *Knickerbocker Holiday*. The play ran for 739 performances on Broadway and drew crowds to companies in Chicago and on the West Coast. A film sale resulted in a popular 1942 release by Warner Brothers starring Monty Woolley as Whiteside and Mary Wickes as the beleaguered nurse, Miss Preen. These two actors had originally created their roles in the Broadway production. *The Man Who Came to Dinner* has sustained its popularity for decades, and it continues to be one of the most frequently produced plays of the American theater.

Woollcott had decided not to play Whiteside in the original production, but once the play was a success he wanted his chance at the role. He starred in the third company that opened in California. Woollcott was a star attraction in himself, so the San Francisco run was sold out for all six weeks. It was during this part of the tour that Woollcott suffered a severe heart attack. But by December of 1940, after an absence of eight months, he returned to the third company to resume his role.

Kaufman and Hart were lionized by the news media. Kaufman appeared on the 20 November 1939, cover of *Time* magazine. The story points out that "only once in the history of the English-speaking theatre has one man been a partner in two firms that have both become household names. In the 1920s, the best-known playwriting partnership in the U.S. was that of Kaufman and Connelly. In the 1930s it has been that of Kaufman and Hart." The opinion expressed in the article regards the plays of Kaufman and Hart as better fused because "the two men are cut to much the same pattern." The *Playbill* elaborates on this idea: "They both have the same kind of humor, they both wear outrageous neckties, and they both have farms in the Bucks County Literary Playground. . . ."[11] Kaufman, touted as the playwright with the highest percentage of successes in the theater as of 1939, was heralded as the King of Broadway.

The Bucks County Trauma

It is never easy to attain success repeatedly in the theater, and circumstances seemed to line up the odds against another Kaufman and
Hart box office sensation for the 1940–41 season. Kaufman had a number of personal concerns regarding the health of both his parents.
Joseph and Nettie Kaufman were in their eighties in 1940, and their
health was deteriorating rapidly. The joy of seeing their son gain international acclaim and become an American household name was
theirs before they both died in the first year of the new decade.

Hart began working on a play by himself. This was the first time
since 1934 that he undertook a nonmusical script without his partner.
Hart felt the need to test his talent solo, but by June, Kaufman and
Hart settled down to write their fall production. Working at Hart's
Fair View Farm in Bucks County, Pennsylvania, inspired them to write
about the struggles that were endured while renovating country
properties.

Their play, *George Washington Slept Here,* focuses on a middle-aged
Manhattan couple as new Bucks County farm owners. Newton Fuller,
in a moment of historical nostalgia, purchased an abandoned Bucks
County stone farmhouse that dates from the revolutionary period. He
brings his wife Annabelle, his daughter Madge, and her friend Steve
to see the house prior to announcing his purchase. Annabelle is neither
thrilled nor charmed with this wreck of a dwelling. Nevertheless, the
Fullers arrive with all their barrels of furnishings a month after their
first visit, fully expecting the house to be renovated. They quickly
learn the disadvantages of country life: no water, road rights are ques-
tionable, trees need maintenance, the roof leaks, and so on. A sudden
storm brings additional problems as two strangers stop for shelter.
They are actors at the local summer stock company; he is the leading-
man type named Clayton Evans and the woman is his wife, Rena Les-
lie, the stock company's leading lady.

Act 2 takes place two months later. The house is restored except
that there still is no water because a successful well has not been
drilled. Life is not as tranquil as Fuller had imagined it would be. Rena
calls on Annabelle to inform her that Madge is attracted to her husband
Clayton. When Newton hears this tale he refuses to believe it. The
weekend at hand promises to bring several invited guests: wealthy Uncle Stanley, Steve, plus four other friends invited by Madge. Also a few
surprises are in store—the latest drilling that finally struck water is on

the neighbor's property; the Fullers are about to lose their country home to the bank; Uncle Stanley is not rich; and Madge is about to run away with Clayton. The Fullers are surrounded by chaos.

Act 3 is the morning after all these discoveries were made. It is bleak for Annabelle and Newton, even though both of them have come to fully appreciate the house and its environs. They begin to drown their sorrows in alcohol. The drinking eventually includes anyone who comes into the room. During the binge Annabelle remembers the clause allowing the property to revert to its previous owners "in its original condition." She easily organizes the inebriated band to destroy the house. Madge, who was stopped from ruining her life, has been taking a walk with Steve. They return from their walk to tell the Fullers some good news for a change. The original map of the land shows that the road and operating well belong to them. Some fancy acting by Uncle Stanley and the others soon convinces the villainous neighbor to help the Fullers save their home.

The play received mixed reviews after the opening on 18 October 1940, and was only moderately successful with a 173-performance run. Atkinson succinctly summarizes the general reaction to the play (*New York Times,* 19 October 1940): "The intellectuals always suspect Mr. Kaufman and Mr. Hart of spreading their comedies thin and of using hackneyed plot devices. Whether they do or not is not a matter of importance if the results are entertaining. But this time the charges fit. For the introductory act is routine wise-cracking, and the plot, when it arrives late in the evening, reaches to the bottom of the barrel for the old mortgage sequence." He concludes the paragraph with a point that still seems strikingly apparent: "Mr. Kaufman and Mr. Hart have gone through the motions of playwriting without taking much fresh enjoyment in what they are doing." The country would await Kaufman and Hart to redeem themselves with another classic comedy, but the partnership had ended.

The situation in *George Washington Slept Here* evolves from a specific locale. Unfortunately, the characters are underdeveloped and remain subordinate to the situation that ceases to be amusing. The craft of the playwrights is evident, but the play falters due in part to the lack of any astounding idiosyncratic characters that had become one of the Kaufman and Hart comedic trademarks.

While the play falters after act 1 as the situation just whirs along its path, it deteriorates in the act 3 scene of violence. Destruction is one of the accepted tools of farce. However, the characters in this play—even in their intoxicated state—are blatant destroyers. Their actions do not create hilarious mayhem: rather they spell out vandalism. While the destruction scene may have been inserted to liven up the script with farcical shtick, it accentuates the negative, thereby confusing the audience reaction. Goldstein observes that this scene "struck a note that was, and remains, sour, if not repellent."[12]

After the Broadway production closed on 15 March 1941, the stock rights were made available. As a result, *George Washington Slept Here* was the most popular new play on the 1941 eastern summer stock circuit. Film rights were sold to Warner Brothers; their 1942 screen version stars Jack Benny and Ann Sheridan.

George Washington Slept Here is the last major play written by Kaufman and Hart, for each playwright drifted into his own separate commitments. An interview with Hart dated 3 February 1941, offers his explanation to the public and perhaps to Kaufman: "One reason for writing *Lady in the Dark* [his own successful play produced January 1941] was my increasing disinterest for plays with plots; for what is known as 'the well-made play.'" In the next paragraph he continues, "Another reason is that over the last few years I've literally sabotaged every serious idea I've had for a play. And so my psychoanalyst made me resolve that the next idea I had, whether it was good or lousy, I'd carry through. This was my next idea [*Lady in the Dark*], and it was about the toughest one I've ever had to realize." His next paragraph underscores his intent: "And now, as the result of "Lady's" success, and my own trend along a path of playwriting that isn't George Kaufman's metier, I can afford not to feel obligated to write a play every year, or to continue to work with George just for the sake of collaborating with him." Hart then pays tribute to Kaufman as "the swellest person I know, and I haven't broken with him one single bit."[13]

Hart's career continued him on a separate path, and he wrote four more plays following *Lady in the Dark.* In time he and Kaufman wrote a few sketches together to support the war effort in some manner. One sketch was created for soldiers to perform.

Dream On, Soldier appeared in the September 1943 issue of *Theatre Arts* magazine. The three-page script recounts a dream that Private Sam Baker is having one night. Baker, from Mapleton, Ohio (the location of *The American Way*), dreams that the war is suddenly declared ended. Upon his return to Mapleton, he is celebrated for participating in the war effort and as a result is given a furnished house, a job with good pay at the bank, and the banker's daughter in marriage. This dream continues to establish his success at the bank and his sweet revenge on people that held power over him prior to his success. Abruptly his dream ends when the morning bugle sounds. *Dream On, Soldier* is obviously a token contribution that the playwrights felt compelled to make.

The era of Kaufman and Hart comedy and cavalcade ended while the theater public continued to wait and to hope for another play from this famous team. Throughout the late thirties and into the early forties, Kaufman and Hart refined a style of sophisticated, urbane wit and social satire that enjoyed its heyday. Other playwrights were influenced by their style, but no imitators wrote plays that are remembered pieces. Kaufman and Hart's names have remained bonded in our minds and frequently their separate endeavors are forgotten. Their legacy is eight plays of which three are American classics.

Chapter Six
Life after Two Pulitzer Prizes

Kaufman entered the decade of the forties as Mr. Broadway, and other laurels were yet to come. One major tribute was paid during the summer of 1941 by the Pasadena Playhouse in California, a nationally renowned regional theater and school established in 1918. The management of this prestigious theater decided to devote a season to plays by George S. Kaufman, beginning with *Beggar on Horseback*, followed by *George Washington Slept Here*, *Dinner at Eight*, *Minick*, *Once in a Lifetime*, *You Can't Take it with You*, *Royal Family*, and *The Man Who Came to Dinner*. The Kaufman season was a box office success for the playhouse, and for Kaufman it reiterated his importance as a contributor to American drama.

While Kaufman prospered, armies moved to the edges of the battlefields where World War II would be fought. Nearly everyone realized it was merely a matter of time before the United States would be engaged in the fighting. Kaufman devoted an increasing amount of time and energy to war-related theatrical charities and benefit performances. But his need to write plays for Broadway productions still had to be fulfilled.

The War Years

In 1940 Edna Ferber had an idea for a play set in Saratoga Springs, New York, a spa-resort that had been the height of fashion for Victorian society. She tried to interest Kaufman in her concept, but after a December visit to the deserted resort, it was evident the subject held no interest for him. Eventually Ferber turned her idea into a novel titled *Saratoga Trunk*.

By mid–1941, Kaufman and Ferber were at work on a play entitled *The Land is Bright*. The title, Ferber acknowledges, was taken from a poem by Arthur Clough:

> And not by eastern windows only,
> When daylight comes, comes in the light,
> In front the sun climbs, slow, how slowly,
> But westward, look, the land is bright. [1]

Malcolm Goldstein mentions that the title was intended to pay homage to Winston Churchill since he had quoted the poem in a speech delivered April 1941. [2] The title has an optimistic ring for a world in turmoil because it was a call for the American people to "Wake up! Wake up!" so all would be saved. [3] *The Land Is Bright* is a melodrama concerned with the rise and fall of three generations of a nouveau-riche American family living in New York City from 1896 to 1941.

The plot centers on the wealthy Kincaid family members who remain still fairly unpolished despite their attempts at storming New York society and its cultural institutions. The year is 1896, and New Yorkers of position remain indifferent to the Kincaids' huge Fifth Avenue mansion and other pretensions. While Ellen Kincaid manipulates a marriage for her daughter Tana with a titled, indigent European, son Grant marries a trollop, and husband Lacey negotiates his takeover of a railroad during the McKinley era as he continues his acts of plundering. Lacey completes his last shady deal while his family departs for an evening at the opera. Lacey's departure for the opera is interrupted when his former partner unexpectedly arrives from out west. The partner, whom Lacey has cheated several times, shoots the robber baron and mortally wounds him.

Twenty-five years elapse between acts. Grant now heads the next generation of Kincaids who are bent on living a decadent existence: Grant's wife Flora spends her life traveling and shopping for clothes; his daughter Linda squanders her time in speakeasies, consorting with gangsters just for thrills; his son Wayne travels and indulges himself with cheap women; his youngest son Teddy is expelled from college; his sister Tana collects titled European husbands; and his mother mourns the ways of her offsprings. Linda's desire for excitement brings tragedy into the family home. After her gangster boyfriend murders someone, he tries to elude the police, and kills Teddy when the youngster defies him.

Twenty years later the family gathers for Grant's seventieth birthday celebration. They have become concerned citizens who hope to serve the United States in a patriotic way, and the family is no longer held in the grip of dissipation. Every member is a respectable, responsible citizen, including Linda, whose youth was shattered by the tragedy she helped create. The realities of the world situation are made painfully clear to this family when Tana's son, who has spent his life in Europe, is liberated from a concentration camp and allowed to come to the United States. The realities of European life in 1941 are brought home to the Kincaids. The experience of seeing Tana's tortured son is more devastating than were their earlier personal tragedies.

The Land Is Bright was produced by Max Gordon. Sam Harris, who had produced Kaufman's scripts since *The Cocoanuts* (1925), had died in July 1941. Kaufman had greatly respected Harris's honesty and dependability, so the playwright turned to Max Gordon, who possessed these same attributes. Gordon had worked with Harris and Kaufman for the past decade, and he was the logical successor to Harris.

Max Gordon recalls, in his autobiography, Kaufman's initial proposal: "Max, Edna and I have completed *The Land Is Bright,* and we would like to have you produce it. Edna and I have eighty per cent between us, and you can have the remainder. It will mean a great deal of prestige for you—doing a play by Edna and me—even if it isn't a hit."[4]

After the production closed, Gordon says, "The outcome was a loose arrangement between us to work together. He (George) received half of my interest in any show he wrote or brought to me for which there was outside financing. When I put up money, so did he. We had no contract, George not being interested in such formalities. And that is the way it was for twenty or so remaining years of his life."[5] Unfortunately, *The Land Is Bright* was not a success, but Gordon felt compensated for it by becoming Kaufman's producer.

Ferber remembers that *The Land Is Bright* was "Powerfully written, in parts, by two people who wanted terribly to say something that they deeply felt should be said. Perhaps that was its chief fault."[6] But during 1941 there had been a number of well-meaning plays including Lillian Hellman's *Watch on the Rhine*—winner of the New York Drama Critics Circle Award, Maxwell Anderson's *Candle in the Wind,* and Fritz Rotter and Allen Vincent's *Letters to Lucerne.* These plays, while well written, were not popular with theatergoers. Perhaps Ferber's observation was correct: the theme was prematurely born and not truly understood.[7]

The Land Is Bright opened on 28 October 1941, and closed after seventy-nine performances. Mixed reviews and the seriousness of the subject seemed to account for the poor box office returns. The play is a flawed piece, particularly in acts 2 and 3 when it is less interesting and not as well written as the first act. Brooks Atkinson's review in the *New York Times* (29 October) claims *The Land Is Bright* "includes the most exciting first act of the season, a mettlesome second act with a little shooting and a final curtain line that is likely to upset your equanimity a good deal." The line referred to is said by Lacey, Grant's grandson, who has just enlisted in the armed forces: "Don't worry, Grandpa. We'll fix it."

The United States entered World War II on 7 December 1941, after the air attack on Pearl Harbor. Kaufman continued his war-effort, fund-raising work; signed a contract with Warner Brothers to write, direct, and produce three motion pictures; directed several Broadway productions; and stopped writing plays for Broadway. The 1942–43 theater season was the first one since 1921, when *Dulcy* was produced, that did not feature a new Kaufman play.

Seven years after its publication in 1937, Max Gordon read J. P. Marquand's Pulitzer Prize-winning novel *The Late George Apley*. It occurred to Gordon that this story about a Boston gentleman who is set in his upper-class manners would make an excellent play. He urged Kaufman to read the novel and to consider its prospects as a theater piece. Kaufman did become interested in the project and agreed to collaborate with Marquand on the adaptation, which they planned to have ready for fall 1944.

Kaufman and Marquand worked throughout the summer on their script, completing it in August. Their efforts resulted in a play, also titled *The Late George Apley,* that bears a partial resemblance to the novel. The action of the play covers an eight-day period in the life of George Apley, while the novel traces his entire lifetime.

The year is 1912, and the scene is the Apley family gathering for Thanksgiving dinner. George Apley, a pillar of Boston society, is set in his ways and in the mores of his New England background. He hopes to be elected president of the Bird Watchers Society; he wants his son John to marry cousin Agnes, who lives next door; and he is upset that cousin Hattie has been buried near his area in the family cemetery. These are all concerns in George's life, which begin to shuffle themselves into events that grow beyond his control.

An unanticipated problem introduces itself on this fine Thanksgiving morning: his daughter Eleanor is developing a love interest in a guest lecturer at Harvard who is not from Boston and, even worse, a graduate of Yale. Then, to make matters more complicated, Apley discovers that John has fallen in love with a girl from Worcester whose father is in the tool-and-die business. George's world is breaking apart because of his children when he is told that the Bird Watchers Society elected someone else president. It seems that George's recent behavior had been thought foolish, and details concerning the cousin Hattie matter became known to various members of the society.

George, in an effort to change his behavior, tries to accommodate the wishes of each family member, but after several conciliatory gestures, he realizes these attempts are in vain since one cannot change one's station in life.

The epilogue takes place thirty years later in 1942, upon the death of Apley. John meets his Uncle Roger Newcombe at the Berkeley Club. From their conversation, it is discovered that John married cousin Agnes as his father desired, but Eleanor married her professor and moved away from Boston. It is now that John finally expresses his appreciation of Apley's ways; he is striving to follow in his father's footsteps.

When *The Late George Apley* opened in New York on 21 November after a successful tryout tour, the enthusiastic reviews guaranteed a long run that lasted for 384 performances. The play provided an amiable evening of comedy and nostalgia, which afforded audiences a respite from the daily traumas of a world at war. The play itself is a bit uneven, particularly in act 2 when a few scenes lapse into extended talkiness, but Kaufman's direction and Leo G. Carroll's acting in the role of George Apley seemed to conceal many of the lesser moments.

A successful tour followed the closing of the Broadway production, and the script was purchased by Twentieth Century-Fox. The film was released in 1947, with Ronald Colman starring as George Apley.

During the fall of 1944 George S. Kaufman was busy with two projects in addition to *The Late George Apley*. He was working on an adaptation of Gilbert and Sullivan's *H.M.S. Pinafore* as well as writing a sketch for a new revue entitled *Seven Lively Arts*. This revue was produced by Billy Rose, who planned to open the show on 7 December as a "commemoration and denial of Pearl Harbor." Rose had recently purchased the old Ziegfeld Theatre, which had been made into a cinema in 1932, after Florenz Ziegfeld's death. Rose refurbished it before restoring its original name for his gala *Seven Lively Arts* production.

The revue, initially planned as a gentle satire on show business and the allied trades, became a gigantic spectacle with sketches by Moss

Hart, Ben Hecht, Charles Sherman, George S. Kaufman, and others; music by Cole Porter; music for a ballet by Igor Stravinsky; and murals in the lobby by Salvador Dali. The idea evolved into an exploration of a wide spectrum of the arts, ranging from ballet and opera to modern painting. The outcome seems to have been more show business pizzazz, but less art than was originally envisioned.

Kaufman's sketch "Local Boy Makes Good" chides stagehands who hate theater, hate scenery, and desire to spend their working hours playing pinochle. The scene is set in producer Jack Martin's office, where he is casting his next production. Mr. Clark, an agent, arrives to see Martin and informs him that he no longer handles actors because the big money is in representing stagehands. Clark sells Martin on the idea of interviewing and auditioning Spike Kennedy, who, despite his reputation as an excellent stagehand, lacks the necessary skills. His audition leaves Martin's office in a shambles.

Spike was played by comedian Bert Lahr, who received good notices for his role. Kaufman's sketch was well received, and the *Seven Lively Arts* production enjoyed a run of 183 performances.

After *Seven Lively Arts* opened, Kaufman returned to work on his satirical musical about life in a Hollywood studio. He had been inspired to write this script in 1942, while playing bridge. One of the other players began to sing a parody of some lines from Gilbert and Sullivan's *H.M.S. Pinafore*: "He nodded his head and never said no, / And now he's head of the studio."

Kaufman spent the winter of 1944–45 working on his version of "Pinafore," titled *Hollywood Pinafore, or The Lad Who Loved A Salary.* Kaufman wrote the book and lyrics, but in the credits added "with deepest apologies to W. S. Gilbert." The plot focuses on Joe Porter, who is head of Pinafore Picture Studio in Hollywood. He is in love with beautiful Brenda Blossom, the star of the studio. She is secretly in love with a lowly screenwriter named Ralph Rackstraw, who only earns seventy-five dollars per week. Porter spends his time discovering future screen stars behind nearly every desk in the studio. Ralph—who is kept as a prisoner in the studio—speaks of his love to Brenda, but she must reject him since he is below her station in life. Ralph is dejected and decides to shoot himself, but Brenda stops him with her confession of love. They vow to wed that very evening.

Director Mike Corcoran, Brenda's father, is fearful that his own career at Pinafore Pictures will be terminated if Brenda does not marry Porter. Corcoran shares his thoughts and fears with Louhedda Hopson, a Hollywood columnist syndicated in 530 newspapers. While these two conspirators try to save the situation, agent Dick Live-eye works against everyone at the studio. His plotting begins to reap dividends because within a short while Porter loses his next picture "The Raven"; Brenda loses Ralph; and Ralph is locked in the studio doghouse. All these events force Louhedda to confess that long ago she made a mistake in her column: when she reported the studio assignments, she reversed the names while copying the news for her column. Porter was supposed to be the writer, and Ralph the head of the studio. As a result of her confession, Ralph takes over the studio, regains the rights for "The Raven," and restores Mike Corcoran as director of the film. Brenda and Ralph plan to wed, Mike proposes to Louhedda, and Porter—now a lowly seventy-five-dollar-a-week writer—decides to marry his former secretary Hebe. A triple wedding with separate honeymoons is planned. The chorus, singing in celebration of the happy outcomes, includes apologies to Gilbert and Sullivan.

Hollywood Pinafore, which retains the music by Sir Arthur Sullivan and the story structure of the original operetta, opened 31 May 1945. It had a run of fifty-two performances due to modest reviews. Lewis Nichols in his *New York Times* review (1 June 1945) says that *"Hollywood Pinafore* shows zest only once in a while; it is one of those musicals which seem never to get fully under way." Two paragraphs later Nichols expresses the criticism that ran through many other columns: Kaufman seemed held back because he kept within Gilbert's plot structure. Kaufman later agreed with this point about staying too close to Gilbert's book. Another problem with this work is that Kaufman's views on Hollywood and screenwriters had been widely known since the 1920s. Therefore, there was little that was new in *Hollywood Pinafore,* and the topic seemed passé.

After the musical closed, Kaufman did not take on any directing assignments or playwriting endeavors. He, like many other Americans, became absorbed with the news during the closing days of World War II. Finally, the surrender of Japan on 14 August 1945 ended the war.

Eventually Kaufman was coaxed into rehearsals as the director of a Max Gordon production. Gordon had decided to offer a dour play about death written by Mary Chase, who had won much praise the season before for *Harvey,* a delightful comedy that enjoyed a run of 1,775 performances. Her new play, *The Next Half Hour,* was written before *Harvey* and was not nearly as strong.

It was during a rehearsal of Chase's opus that Kaufman received devastating news: Beatrice Kaufman, whose health had not been good during the fall of 1945, suddenly died. Her death from a cerebral hemorrhage on 6 October, was an unexpected shock to everyone. At her funeral service held two days later, publisher Bennett Cerf's eulogy expressed the feelings of her many friends: "Beatrice Kaufman's love of life and laughter, her abiding interest in the affairs of a myriad of friends, were so great that it will be a long time before they realize she is gone. She was the core and the connecting link of scores of people in every walk of life who owe some of their success today to her ever-ready counsel and sympathy when the going was roughest. Part of the fun of doing things was telling Beatrice about them. Her death will leave an unfillable gap in our lives."[8]

Life without Beatrice would be very difficult for George S. Kaufman. She had provided him with comfortable, attractive homes, had been his trusted critic and friend, and had added a social context to his life beyond the theater and the bridge table. Their relationship, while unconventional, was one with mutual strong bonds and dependencies. After her death he believed that he could never work again.

Somehow Kaufman went through the motions of conducting the remaining rehearsals for *The Next Half Hour,* but the emphasis on death in the script certainly could not have provided any escape from his own pain. The play opened on 29 October and closed after eight performances. Suddenly Kaufman was idle, without projects and without Beatrice, but with time to face his sorrow and his sense of loss.

Trying to Pick Up the Pieces

During the winter of 1945–46 Kaufman suggested to movie screenwriter and producer Nunnally Johnson that they collaborate on a musical inspired by one of Johnson's short stories written in the 1930s. Johnson, one of Hollywood's most prolific, highly respected writers, accepted the Kaufman invitation. Arthur Schwartz was selected to compose the music, and Ira Gershwin provided the lyrics. This team was composed of very talented individuals who would surely create an entertaining musical.

The title of their musical comedy is *Park Avenue,* and work on the book and score was concentrated into the summer of 1946 with the idea of staging the production for the fall. Kaufman's only major diversion was the 1 August wedding of Moss Hart to Kitty Carlisle, just prior to Kaufman's first rehearsal for *Park Avenue.*

The action for *Park Avenue* is set on the estate of Mrs. Ogden (Sybil) Bennett, who resides on fashionable Long Island. Undoubtedly she must have a town abode on Park Avenue or at least can afford one. Otherwise there is no relationship to the title in the play. Mrs. Bennett's daughter Madge invites Ned Scott, her fiancé from Charleston, South Carolina, to the estate in order to meet her parents. When Ned, a southern gentleman with southern ideas about manners and morality, discovers that Sybil has been married four times—and that her three ex-husbands with their current wives are coming to meet him—he is astounded and distressed. Shortly after everyone arrives, Sybil announces her intentions to divorce Mr. Bennett and marry a fifth husband. This sets off a series of divorce and remarriage plans for every member of the parental group. Madge takes this news in stride, but Ned, who is greatly distressed by the conduct of Madge's multiple sets of parents, "marches away" from the house.

When Ned has not returned to the house by 8:00 P.M., Madge is troubled. Sybil decides to make a sacrifice for Madge's future happiness: she will stay married to her present husband, Ogden Bennett. This means that everyone else must also remain married to his or her present mate instead of proceeding with the exchanges that were planned. When Ned returns and accepts the gestures of marital stability, his marriage proposal to Madge is back on track. However, Ned cancels their marriage plans again because one ex-husband failed to realize the moratorium on new mates was agreed upon, and he announces his engagement. This dilemma is corrected by Sybil, who then arranges to trick Ned into marrying Madge immediately before he changes his mind again. Ned accepts his new marital arrangement with alacrity.

The flaws in *Park Avenue* were beyond being masked by good casting, brilliant direction, opulent sets, and gorgeous costumes. The authors of the book misjudged the mood of the audience following World War II: the play's cynical view of life, devoid of any genuine warmth, was not welcomed by a nation whose heroes wanted to return to a pleasant, untroubled existence. The characters in *Park Avenue* were spoiled, privileged people who seemed to contribute nothing to society. While the characters and their marital shenanigans would have been amusing in the 1930s, their problems and interests were insignificant given the condition of the world. They did not provide mirth, just emptiness.

The musical's unfavorable reviews were based primarily on the book.

The topic of divorce was thought to be belabored; the book was criticized for being too long and wordy. Brooks Atkinson in his *New York Times* review (5 November 1946) summarizes the play in three words: "thin, disdainful and general." The production had a seventy-two performance run, and its closing left Kaufman even more depressed. He had reportedly realized that the show was in trouble before it opened in New York on 4 November, but in his state of mind he was unable to do major revisions.

Kaufman did not undertake any additional projects for the rest of the 1946–47 theater season. While he was still trying to come to grips with his personal grief, new American playwrights were beginning to build reputations and to change the course of the drama. Tennessee Williams had established his presence on Broadway in 1945 with *The Glass Menagerie* and grew in stature as a playwright in 1947 with *A Streetcar Named Desire,* which was the winner of the Pulitzer Prize for drama. In the same year Arthur Miller had his first Broadway success with *All My Sons,* which he followed in February 1949 with *Death of a Salesman,* winner of the Pulitzer Prize for that season. The works of these two men, who emerged as the next generation of major American playwrights, were rooted in different American realities and visions than was Kaufman's drama. These postwar dramas were not the type of plays Kaufman would have been asked either to rewrite or to direct. For the first time in more than twenty-five years George S. Kaufman played no part whatsoever in the creation of innovative American theater.

When Nunnally Johnson offered Kaufman the opportunity to direct a film in 1947 at Universal Studio, the invitation provided what appeared to be a new challenge for Kaufman. He had never directed a film, and his project was a script written by Charles MacArthur titled *The Senator Was Indiscreet.* It is a story about a mediocre, dull United States senator who blackmails his way into being nominated as the presidential candidate of his party.

Once Kaufman began working in Hollywood, he realized that directing a play for the theater was very different from directing a film. He disliked not being totally responsible for the final effect of the product. A film is ultimately in the hands of an editor who determines its shape and scope. Kaufman also did not enjoy the film because of the manner in which it is shot: often scenes are filmed out of sequence, and most scenes require numerous retakes punctuated by other interruptions.

The Senator Was Indiscreet was released in December 1947, and it proved to be unpopular. Despite other problems with the film, it seems that once again Kaufman and Johnson had put their efforts behind a vehicle with an unacceptable topic. It was now out of fashion to satirize the workings of the federal government and the makings of a president. And with the first hearings of the House Un-American Activities Committee, in October 1947, the film could even have been interpreted as un-American.

Kaufman returned from Hollywood in August 1947 and soon considered another collaboration with Edna Ferber, who was between novels. They commenced their playwriting project titled *Bravo!* in 1948. Kaufman also kept himself occupied with a directing project titled *Town House,* which would open the week prior to his first *Bravo!* rehearsal on the following Monday morning. It seemed that George S. Kaufman was back in his old stride.

Kaufman and Ferber first considered the idea of a play about refugees in 1941, but dismissed it. Ferber claims she became obsessed with the idea of writing about a group of Europeans relocated to New York.[9] Her obsession developed in part as a reaction to the policy of restricted immigration imposed by the United States government. Also, it was those people who had come to the United States that haunted her: the strangers in a strange land that were recognizable by "their eyes, the walk, the set of the shoulders, the absence of that certain cockiness which your accustomed American habitually wears all the way from the day laborer to the corporation president."[10] Kaufman was not keen on the idea of a play about refugees, but Ferber convinced him of its merits.

The European refugees in the plot of *Bravo!* are mainly artists—with a sprinkling of titled nobility—who are trying to survive the trauma of establishing their lives in a new country. The refugees include a celebrated continental playwright named Zoltan Lazko who discovers his scripts are now considered old-fashioned; his wife Rosa Rucker, who is a famous actress not able to find work in American theater; and a number of other famous Europeans now living in reduced circumstances working at jobs such as taxi driver, waitress, and salesperson. They live as a mutually dependent family in an old, shabby brownstone house on New York's West Side. The group is increased by one when Lisa Kemper, daughter of an actor friend of Zoltan and Rosa's, arrives from England, where she was in a nursing home for several months suffering from the cruelties of a war-torn life.

Within two months Lisa is an integrated member of the household. Kurt, working as taxi driver, is in love with her, and they are planning to marry. It is at this juncture that the jealous Vilna Prager, a former ballerina whom Kurt fished out of the river, sets the wheels of the Immigration and Naturalization Department in motion. Two agents visit the house to question Lisa and Zoltan too, for he served as her sponsor in the United States. The agents are appeased after the interview, and even more good luck rains down upon Lisa when she is cast in a Broadway play.

The last act revolves around Lisa's Broadway debut, which will take place that evening. The conflict is that the immigration agents plan to detain Lisa and Zoltan following the performance. Earlier that day, while Zoltan had been sitting in the park, he fortuitously had met a gentleman who seemed to be important. The man liked Zoltan and gave him his telephone number, even though Zoltan did not know the man's name. Since Zoltan is now confronted with the prospect of deportation, he calls his new friend for advice. The man turns out to be Bernard Baruch, the famous financier and government adviser, who promises Zoltan that he will intercede if Lisa and Zoltan's cases stand as explained. The future begins to take on a rosy glow of hope and promise for most of the residents of this unusual household. Their talents are being discovered in their new country, and they are adjusting to their new lives. Even Zoltan begins to consider writing a play that is about America.

The model for Zoltan was immediately recognizable to New York theatergoers as Ferenc Molnar, the Hungarian dramatist who in 1940 had become an American citizen. Molnar's most famous play *Liliom* written in 1909 was the basis of the musical *Carousel* written in 1945 by Rogers and Hammerstein. Lili Darvas, Molnar's wife in real life, was cast as Rosa Rucker, a role the actress knew how to portray without being sentimental. When *Bravo!* opened at the Lyceum Theatre in New York on 11 November 1948, Lili Darvas received glowing reviews, but the play did not.

The penetrating analysis made by Brooks Atkinson in his *New York Times* review (12 November 1948), speaks to the subject matter of *Bravo!*: "All things considered, this is one of the most vital subjects of our time, laden with all sorts of human qualities from tragic to comic and from gallant to pathetic." He continues by praising the respect Ferber and Kaufman have for the civilized victims of a great cultural disaster, but concludes that "*Bravo!* skips quickly over the surface of a

subject that needs greater insight and profounder convictions."
Though the play "recognizes the many tangible and intangible problems of the refugees it is portraying, it does not get much beyond
recognition."

This uneven play becomes weaker after act 1 because the characters
lack development, and the plot becomes forced, which obviously affects the manner in which the topic is explored. *Bravo!* was closed by
producer Max Gordon after its forty-fourth performance. The failure of
this play seemed to thrust Ferber and Kaufman into different professional directions. She believed the failure of *Bravo!* generated the desire
to write her Texas novel, *Giant.* This carried her into the next project,
her Alaskan novel, *Ice Palace.* Kaufman and Ferber remained good
friends, even though their theater partnership that had spanned
twenty-four years quietly expired.

Kaufman was greatly affected by the failure of *Bravo!* since it was
coupled with another nonsuccess, the even shorter twelve-performance
run of *Town House,* a production that he had directed. He began to
believe that his theatrical instincts were deserting him. But as Kaufman contemplated this dilemma, his reputation as a wit was already
carrying him down another career path when *Bravo!* closed.

Other Beginnings

In the fall of 1948 Kaufman agreed to appear on a radio panel show
called "This is Broadway." He served as one of the three panelists who
advised various show-business guests about their special, individual,
nonserious problems, and his verbal adroitness made Kaufman popular
with home audiences. The program became so successful that in 1949
CBS decided to move it to television. The new television panel show
named "This is Show Business" included George S. Kaufman, who at
the age of sixty would become a television personality.

Another new start in Kaufman's life was his marriage to British
actress Leueen MacGrath. This occurred before the radio program became a weekly television event. The actress, twenty-six years Kaufman's junior, had been working in theater since her debut in England
in 1933. She had come to New York in the fall of 1948, to perform
her first role in the United States in the hit play *Edward, My Son.* She
received rave notices in the role of Eileen Perry. Kaufman and Mac-
Grath met formally for the first time at a small dinner party he gave
for his close married friends Garson Kanin and Ruth Gordon. Since

Leueen MacGrath was a guest of the Kanins', Kaufman insisted that she should be part of the gathering. Kaufman and MacGrath became a Broadway item, but no one seemed to believe their relationship was more than a casual affair. It, therefore, came as a complete surprise when Kaufman announced that he and Leueen would be married on 26 May 1949. Life had taken several new turns for Kaufman as he entered the decade of the fifties.

Chapter Seven

Trials and Triumphs of the Fifties

Nineteen-fifty marked a year of happiness on a personal level for George S. Kaufman, but professionally his career was at its nadir. He had not written a successful full-length play since *The Late George Apley* was staged for the 1944–45 season, and he had not directed a winning production. It appeared as if his talent had been consumed after being involved with eight nonsuccessful productions.

Collaborating with Leueen

One day Kaufman asked Leueen if she would consider collaborating with him on a play. She agreed, and they began to consider plot ideas in May 1950 while sailing to Europe. When they returned to New York on 1 August, they had a draft of their script to share with Max Gordon. Kaufman wanted to move ahead with plans for the play he was working on with Leueen, but he had accepted a commitment to direct a musical production named *Guys and Dolls* that was to start rehearsals on 6 September.

When the musical opened on 24 November, it was immediately heralded as a hit. Kaufman's work earned him the Antoinette Perry Award, usually referred to as the Tony, for best direction. *Guys and Dolls* ran for three years on Broadway, playing for 1,200 performances. Kaufman's theatrical skills were once again lauded by the critics.

Buoyed by this turn of events, he returned to the script written with his wife. *The Small Hours* was selected as the title, and the Broadway opening was set for February 1951. This two-act play written with twenty-six scenes features a large cast of twenty-nine actors plus extras. The story was inspired by a married couple whom Leueen observed during their 1950 voyage to Europe. She speculated that the husband had outgrown the wife intellectually, and on that idea hangs the thread on which the plot was spun.

Henry Mitchell, a prominent publisher, is saddled with his wife Laura, who has become an insecure bundle of nerves. She does not seem capable of coping with most social and personal situations, so she turns secretly to imbibing alcoholic beverages in order to survive. While some of the scenes reveal the saga of this inept housewife, others focus on the Mitchell children. Daughter Dorothy is working her way into a marriage during act 1, while son Peter is heading toward trouble with the police due to his need for marijuana.

Act 2 opens with Laura resting at a seaside Florida hotel following Dorothy's wedding. While Laura is trying to understand herself and become a more independent person, the other members of the family are pursuing their individual recreations: Peter is drifting in the Greek isles, Dorothy is on her honeymoon, and Henry is having an affair with one of his literary clients. After Laura returns to New York, she tries to live a new productive life. She believes she has gained enough courage to ask Henry for a divorce, but the ensuing argument results in her becoming physically paralyzed even though there is no physiological reason for her condition.

The melodrama increases as each member of the family presents another complication. Peter reveals to his mother that he is trying to become a writer, Dorothy has her first argument with her husband, and a man is threatening to take control of Henry's company. These events turn one notch more calamitous: Peter confesses to Laura that his drug problems are related to his latent homosexuality; Henry discovers that his mistress, the author, is deceitful; and Dorothy comes home declaring she is planning to get a divorce. Despite the many traumas, all ends happily after Henry severs his relationship with his mistress and speaks to Laura of his need for her. He also confesses that he wavered from being faithful to her due to his lack of self-confidence. Once Laura realizes she is not the only weak person in the Mitchell family, her paralysis disappears.

The play seems very much in the mode of a television soap opera, for the authors use the cinematographic technique of cutting from one location to another in an attempt to convey simultaneous action. Also, the events within a scene happen so rapidly that the action becomes artificial and ludicrous. The characters are hardly developed, the plot is without depth, and the ideas are shallow. Brooks Atkinson mentions in his *New York Times* review (16 February 1951) that "the authors hardly go to work on a scene before the scenery begins to move." He poses two questions in the concluding paragraph: "But isn't a production like this a substitute for writing? Hasn't the real core of drama been lifted out of the play?" The play relied on its scenery, costumes, and cast to make it work as a theater piece; therefore, it is all show and little real substance.

Topically, the play mentions two societal issues that were taboo subjects when the play was originally presented: the use of marijuana by an upper-middle-class adult, and the confession of homosexual tendencies. Kaufman continues in his role of cultural historian, pointing out the problems encountered by the affluent. He also illustrates that post-World-War-II life abounds with people who are scared, lonely, and seeking support. He does not paint the picture that financial success ensures the American Dream. *The Small Hours* portrait is contrary to the 1950s cliché image of the harvest that wealth will bring. It is too bad that the authors did not prime their canvas better before scrawling in the details.

The Small Hours received poor reviews, and the production lost $120,000 by the time it closed after its twenty-third performance.

Additional Setbacks

During the summer of 1951 the Kaufmans began their second play-writing collaboration. Leueen had suggested a play featuring reincarnation, a topic that would attain popularity by the midfifties. This new script was completed by the end of summer and titled *Fancy Meeting You Again*. The leading role was tailored for Leueen's acting talents, so the couple confidently approached Max Gordon, suggesting a mid-winter Broadway opening.

For the first time Gordon gathered up his courage and refused to produce a Kaufman script. Gordon relied on Kaufman for financial backing, play doctoring, advice, and new scripts, but he had produced *Bravo!* and *The Small Hours* under protest. *Fancy Meeting You Again* struck Gordon as another expensive fiasco. Kaufman had never had such a rebuke. However, another producer surfaced quickly, and plans were made for a mid-winter opening with rehearsals scheduled to being on 25 October.

Prior to that rehearsal date, Kaufman suffered a stroke that affected the left side of his body and the sight in his left eye. Within a month Kaufman was released from the hospital. He had regained significant use of his left side and felt well enough to begin conducting rehearsals on 8 November for *Fancy Meeting You Again*.

The setting for this play is the New York studio of sculptor Amanda Phipps, who is about to be married in a ceremony set amongst her art creations. Suddenly she changes her mind, decides that she is not enough in love with the bridegroom to cleave to him for life. Actually she confesses to her secretary that she has been in love with another man, the same man for five thousand years—through fifteen separate lives—and the real problem is that this man has never married her. After the aborted wedding ceremony, art critic Sinclair Heybore walks into Amanda's life. She immediately recognizes him as the man she has always loved, and she is delighted to have found him in this lifetime. Heybore came to her studio to view her latest statue, which Amanda calls "Big Girl." Neither Heybore nor the committee that commissioned it appreciate this particular piece, but Heybore loves Amanda even though he dislikes her statue.

The dilemma results when Heybore discovers that Amanda believes in reincarnation. His mother is also a believer, and she has driven him to seeing an analyst. Heybore walks out of Amanda's life; the committee refuses to pay for the sculpture; and Amanda receives a call from "The Visitor" who tells her that this is her last life since she has not improved her conduct. Also included in the plot are two segments from Amanda's former lives, one as a Stone Age beauty, and the other as a girl in ancient Rome.

All seems lost for several minutes, but every problem eventually will be settled happily: Amanda will be paid for the statue; Heybore returns to marry her and to take her to Egypt with him since her information regarding an ancient palace seems accurate; and "The Visitor" will obviously be appeased with the happy turn of events.

The critical notices of *Fancy Meeting You Again* seemed to be the most positive when commenting about the acting of a gifted young comedian named Walter Matthau, who played the role of Sinclair Heybore. Leueen's acting did not garner the hoped-for accolades. Brooks Atkinson states in his *New York Times* review (15 January 1952): "But it is feared that her acting is not much more resourceful than the writing." He had referred to the writing of the play earlier in the review by saying that "*Fancy Meeting You Again* seems to have been written at random about characters who necessarily repeat a similar pattern every time they meet as they hop and skip through the centuries." Atkinson believes the play is not up to the standard of anything previously written by Kaufman, and it is simply "not very good." The play closed at the end of the first week after its eighth performance.

Despite the devastating reviews for *Fancy Meeting You Again,* George S. Kaufman remained keen on continuing to collaborate with Leueen. Between 1952 and 1953 they worked on two more scripts that came to naught. The first is a screenplay titled *And Baby Makes Two.* It concerns the family of a country girl named Betty who sets out for New York in order to find the unknown, young artist who is the father of her baby girl. Through the involvement of a television reporter, the citizenry of New York help the family to search for the unknown father. Months later, after he is discovered in Paris, he returns to Betty. The other script is a seventy-four-minute television play titled *The Hat.* This script is reminiscent of *First Lady*: the plot turns on how the rivalry between two ladies affects the outcome of a nominating run for the presidential party candidate by one lady's husband.

It was while Kaufman was collaborating with Leueen on these plays that he faced a new problem. On 21 December 1952, while on the air during a live broadcast of "This is Show Business" Kaufman said, "Let's make this one program where no one sings *Silent Night.*" Many audience members took umbrage with the remark because they believed it was "irreligious" and, therefore, anti-Christian. The complaints concerned the sponsor and the network, so George S. Kaufman was removed from the television program. Individual show-business personalities rallied to his side because they were incensed over the unjust treatment he had received. And in January CBS invited Kaufman to resume his status as a panelist on "This is Show Business." He served in this capacity until May 1953, when other obligations made it necessary for him to leave his role as a weekly television personality. Meanwhile, Max Gordon was interested in broadening Kaufman's playwriting opportunities by introducing him to another possible collaborator.

Back in Stride

Gordon had met Howard Teichmann when the hopeful playwright arrived in the producer's office with both an introduction from an associate of Gordon's and a badly written play.[1] While Gordon was unimpressed with the script, he did believe that Teichmann had the type of talent that could be complementary to George S. Kaufman's abilities. Teichmann had come to New York in the late 1930s and served as stage manager for Orson Welles at the Mercury Theatre. Later, he spent two years writing Welles's radio program "The Mercury Theatre of the Air." Then, following World War II, Teichmann wrote for television and wrote the play that brought him to Max Gordon's attention. Gordon called Kaufman with the request that the playwright meet Teichmann. Kaufman followed the suggestion, and the meeting resulted in a collaboration on a play they titled *The Solid Gold Cadillac*.

A Narrator introduces the play by calling it "a fairy story—the story of Cinderella and the four ugly corporation directors." The plot begins at the fifty-ninth annual meeting of the stockholders of the General Products Corporation of America. This meeting is interrupted by a woman stockholder who asks leading questions regarding the directors' salaries. It turns out that this annoying woman named Mrs. Partridge is an elderly character actress who holds ten shares of stock. In order to protect themselves from Mrs. Partridge's probing questions—which if answered could be embarrassing—the directors hire her to correspond with the small-share stockholders in the corporation. When the directors lament about the lack of governmental contracts, they decide to remedy the situation by sending Mrs. Partridge to Washington, D.C., to talk to McKeever, who was the former Chairman of the Board at General Products prior to assuming his present governmental post. Mrs. Partridge convinces McKeever that General Products needs him to protect the corporation, so he resigns his post and returns with her to New York.

The directors are afraid that they will be demoted if McKeever gets back into the company. In an attempt to regain his corporate position, McKeever takes the company to court on an antilobbying act. Since Mrs. Partridge serves as the star witness for the government's case, she is fired from General Products. However, while she is cleaning out her office and packing her belongings, she reads a letter from a stockholder to McKeever. He realizes that the stockholders are sending their proxies to Mrs. Partridge because her correspondence with them generated their trust. She has enough votes to be in control of the corporation. After assuming her position of control, she fires all the present officers of the company. The last scene in the play is set at the sixtieth annual stockholders' meeting. Mrs. Partridge holds the offices of vice president, secretary, and treasurer while McKeever is president. Her means of transportation to this meeting has been a solid gold Cadillac.

The Solid Gold Cadillac opened on 5 November 1953, at the Belasco Theatre in New York, where it remained through 526 performances. Mrs. Partridge was played by veteran actress Josephine Hull, who was lavishly praised by most of the reviewers. The success of *The Solid Gold*

Cadillac seemed firmly rooted in Josephine Hull's performances. Atkinson attests to her power on stage in his *New York Times* review (6 November 1953) by devoting the first half of the article to lauding her performance. As for the play, he calls it "a graceless, random satire on the knavery of big business." He condemns the authors for not developing ideas and for allowing the satire to gallop off in all directions. Nevertheless, audiences thronged to the theater to enjoy Josephine Hull in *The Solid Gold Cadillac.*

Columbia Pictures bought the film rights and hired Abe Burrows— wit, playwright, and fellow panelist with Kaufman on "This is Show Business"—to write the screenplay. The role of Mrs. Partridge was refashioned for a younger, more attractive actress. The part was given to Academy Award-winning actress Judy Holliday, who was known for her shrewd dumb-blonde role in *Born Yesterday.* Burrows shaped the Partridge character to fit the dumb-blonde stereotype. The film, released in October 1956, also became a hit at the box office.

After the initial success of *The Solid Gold Cadillac,* Kaufman and Teichmann started to write another play. This work, completed early in 1954, was titled "Exile." It is the story of a hunted Czechoslovakian politician named Karl Brock who lives in New York with his wife Karen. Karl has been in exile since the Communist coup of 1948 placed his country under Russian control. Now Communist Emil Svoboda has traced Karl once again, and threatens to kill the exile because he is the only possible leader alive who could lead a rebellion against the current Communist regime. This melodramatic tale, which even includes the United States unofficially attempting to instigate a revolt behind the Iron Curtain, was never produced.

Later in 1954 Kaufman and Teichmann completed another script, titled "In the Money." This comedy is about an unsuccessful insurance man named Sam Watson, who inherits nearly a million dollars. Suddenly his rich, spoiled sisters and their professional husbands begin to treat Sam royally. But when his investments return him to his previous state of poverty, the family ignores him. However, Sam finds himself "in the money" again by the final curtain. Production plans for this play were announced, but they were later postponed by Kaufman, and the play was shelved. Six years later Teichmann began with Kaufman to rework "In the Money"; the ailing senior playwright needed a project.[2] They never completed their polishing of the script.

What is different about "In the Money" is the presentational style of production suggested by the playwrights. They request that the stage be set with three platforms decorated with small railings around them. Actors are instructed to mount these platforms and frequently address their speeches directly to the audience. While this type of presentation was not new in the theater, it was a new approach for Kaufman and showed that he was still interested in experimenting with different theatrical techniques.

What Price Success!

In 1954 producers Cy Feuer and Ernest Martin asked Kaufman to write the book for a musical adaptation of *Ninotchka,* the 1939 film in which Greta Garbo had her first opportunity to appear in a light comedy. Kaufman accepted the assignment after the producers agreed to his condition that allowed Leueen to collaborate with him. Cole Porter was contracted to supply the music and lyrics for the musical, which was titled *Silk Stockings.*

The plot commences as three Russian agents arrive in Paris. Their mission is to collect Peter Ilyitch Boroff, a famous Russian pianist and composer, who is not ready to return to Moscow. The three agents are wined, dined, and provided with attractive female companions by an American named Steve Canfield, who wants the Russians to forget their mission. Canfield is acting as Boroff's theatrical agent, and the American promoter wants to use Boroff's music in a film with which he is involved. A woman commissar named Ninotchka is sent to Paris to return all four comrades to Moscow. A major segment of act 1 is devoted to Ninotchka's transformation from hard-line, no-nonsense Communist party member to romantic female enjoying the frills of Western capitalism, while becoming smitten with the ever-attentive Canfield. Into this plot comes Janice Dayton, American film star who is going to star in Canfield's film project. The plot is further complicated because Boroff becomes infatuated with Dayton.

The motion picture is in production when act 2 moves to a film studio sound stage. Canfield first serenades and then proposes marriage to Ninotchka, who quickly accepts his offer. Then love begins to get mixed up with politics when the Russians become upset with the text of the film. They believe the film is an insult to their country, and since Boroff's music is part of the film, the offense is worse. Ninotchka decides they must all immediately return to Russia.

In act 3 the comrades are back to their Russian routines of life. Ninotchka has been demoted and is currently in charge of a house for agents. The three comrades who were in Paris with her all come to visit their friend, the unhappy, dissatisfied Ninotchka. The trio is also disenchanted with their current lives, when suddenly, in the middle of the mood of depression, comes Canfield. He is happily reunited with Ninotchka just before she receives word that she must face charges of "conspiracy to undermine the government." Apparently, Commissar Marovitch, who is Ninotchka's superior, has trumped up the charge. When Commissar Marovitch arrives at Ninotchka's house, Canfield somehow persuades Marovitch to flee from Russia to America. The commissar arranges for an airplane that will take himself, Ninotckha, Canfield, plus the trio of agents to America.

Silk Stockings had a difficult tryout period, particularly when it opened on 22 November 1954, in Philadelphia. Local critics and audiences voiced their displeasure with the production, so producers Feuer and Martin asked Abe Burrows to see the musical and to offer his reactions. The producers argued with George S. Kaufman over the book, and eventually Kaufman asked Burrows to assist with script changes. Burrows's contributions were significant: his name was added to the credits as an author.

Accounts differ about the rift that transpired between the producers and the Kaufmans—and when it occurred—but the final results are the same: the Kaufmans ceased their work on the book, and George S. Kaufman left his directorial position on *Silk Stockings* due to irreconcilable differences. As Leueen and George were leaving Boston, the second tryout city, Kaufman told reporters that he had been "fired from his own show!" The aggravating events connected with *Silk Stockings* left their mark on Kaufman both emotionally and physically. He had suffered a slight stroke prior to going to Boston. And in a letter written to Abe Burrows after the show opened on Broadway, Kaufman, alluding to a remark that Abe wrote to him, says, "As for the 'crazy ride on a roller coaster,' it was more painful for some of us than others. I would be less than honest if I told you that my own 'scar tissue' has completely healed."[3]

On 24 February 1955 *Silk Stockings* opened in New York to rave reviews. Atkinson in the *New York Times* (26 February 1955) proclaims that *Silk Stockings* "represents the best goods in the American musical comedy emporium." Later in the review he writes that the musical "offers the wittiest dialogue of recent years." The production, which allowed audiences to laugh at Iron Curtain policies and rhetoric, ran for 478 performances. *Silk Stockings* marked the end of two illustrious

Broadway careers: it was Cole Porter's last musical score in a thirty-nine-year career, and it was George S. Kaufman's last play to have a Broadway opening.

Metro-Goldwyn-Mayer purchased the screen rights for producer Arthur Freed. His name was synonymous with the glitter and high quality of the MGM musical, for he was instrumental in the development of screen musicals in the 1940s and 1950s. The successful film released in July 1957 stars Fred Astaire, Cyd Charisse, and Janis Paige.

The Need to Keep Writing

Life became less kind to George S. Kaufman in the years following *Silk Stockings*. Max Gordon continued for a time to find ideas and collaborators for Kaufman, but nothing ever developed from these attempts. Kaufman began to work with Alan Campbell on a musical book called "The Lipstick War." Campbell was a friend of Leueen's, but Kaufman had known him long before Leueen, for Campbell had been married to Dorothy Parker in the days of the Algonquin Round Table lunches.

"The Lipstick War" was in draft stage by May 1956, when Kaufman sailed to England. Months later when Max Gordon read the script, he tried to entice Rogers and Hammerstein to compose a score. After they declined, Gordon lost interest in the project. The musical was never produced, which did not seem to bother Kaufman since he thought the script was not promising. In a letter to Moss and Kitty Hart, Kaufman mentions that the play is "old-fashioned—it is hard to change one's style."[4]

The title page of "The Lipstick War" manuscript states that the idea for the script was "suggested by an article in *The Nation* by Walter Goodman." The plot revolves around the owners of two major cosmetic firms specializing in lipstick. The rivalry between the two companies results in the established firm being merged with the newer one that is presided over by a beautiful woman. She is in love with the man who headed the competing company, and these two executives merge their businesses before they merge their lives in matrimony. The play satirizes advertising methods, government regulations pertaining to antitrust, sons who inherit established corporations, and corporate spying. It has a few glimmers of Kaufman's style, but it spins out its tale too much. Kaufman's assessment was accurate, it is "old-fashioned."

In February 1957 Leueen informed Kaufman that she wanted a divorce. She was acting in a Broadway production of Graham Greene's *The Potting Shed,* which opened in January 1957, so she remained in New York. Leueen visited with Kaufman during their period of separation, and they wrote a one-act play, *Amicable Parting,* which is concerned with a separated couple who need to divide the joint possessions.

Bill and Alice Reynolds bicker continuously while dividing their personal items. As they begin to drink, they reminisce about the better moments from their years together. The couple briefly considers a reconciliation; however, their disputatious natures interfere. Alice angrily departs, leaving Bill in a dejected state. Within a few minutes she returns to the apartment and makes a silent gesture, suggesting a reunion is possible.

The Kaufmans—unlike their characters the Reynolds—did not reunite, but their concern for each other remained strong. *Amicable Parting* was first staged on 14 November 1957, at Columbia Teachers College. The play's first professional production opened on 3 June 1968, at the Off Broadway Playhouse in Camden, New Jersey, where it played during Lunch Theatre for five performances.

During the fall of 1957 George S. Kaufman was involved in directing his last Broadway play, produced by David Merrick, the newly proven talent among Broadway producers. Despite Kaufman's frail health, he believed work was good for him. The script, titled *Romanoff and Juliet,* was the work of English actor/writer Peter Ustinov. The play opened on 10 October 1957, and it was a solid hit that ran for 389 performances.

Kaufman continued to search for new play ideas and new collaborators. Several projects were discussed: some were started, but few were completed. One musical play from 1958, titled "The Same as Before Only Worse," was written with Ruth Goetz. The title page of the manuscript acknowledges Marc Connelly for invaluable assistance and credits lyrics by Carolyn Leigh with music by Cy Coleman.

The story includes the shady maneuvers of Jim Turk, union president, and the general determination of Madame Greco, celebrated opera diva. These disparate characters eventually meet because Turk's union members may not finish the new opera house in time for its premier performance starring Greco. The diva and the union president fall in love. Suddenly love conquers several of Turk and Greco's existing problems, while Turk's shrewdness solves his woes caused by the Senate

Investigating Committee on Labor. Though the script seemed to have promise, the project faded when Ruth Goetz withdrew.

Kaufman's next playwriting project was written with Leueen. This play, "I Give it Six Months," was optioned for production after the script was completed. The plot concerns an English woman poet and her romance with a New York City taxi driver. Before plans for the production of "I Give it Six Months" were underway, Kaufman suffered another stroke in November 1958. His health continued to decline steadily. Friends visited him at his home, and there was talk of more plays and collaborations, but nothing ever evolved into a stage production. George S. Kaufman wrote until he could write no longer. Writing was his life; writing was living.

His death occurred on 2 June 1961, shortly after breakfast. It was a quiet, peaceful end.

The Kaufman Legacy

Our inheritance from George S. Kaufman is the stories that made him a legend in his own time. It is not easy to encapsulate the personality of this unusual man, but Moss Hart reportedly once pointed out that there were many George S. Kaufmans:

There was George the misanthrope, the harsh, metallic, poison-tongued George who, like some ogre out of an old-fashioned fairy tale, could scare people off, the 'wintry and distant George, sad, lonely, remote from his fellow men.' But there was also a loving George, a man who, beneath that jaundiced, craggy facade he presented to the world, could care deeply, could be a determinedly devoted friend, who could be, and was, thoughtful of the needs of others.[5]

Our inheritance from George S. Kaufman is his plays. Some are American classics, comedies that continue to delight audiences everywhere: *Once in a Lifetime, You Can't Take It with You, The Royal Family, The Man Who Came to Dinner, The Solid Gold Cadillac,* and *If Men Played Cards as Women Do.*

And some of his plays do not deserve to gather dust, plays that come alive when presented in a theater, plays that deserve productions: *June Moon, Beggar on Horseback, Dinner at Eight, Butter and Egg Man, Merton of the Movies, Dulcy,* and *The Still Alarm.* There are others—interesting historical theater pieces such as the cavalcade dramas written with Moss

Hart, the farces written for the Marx Brothers, and at least two political satires—*The Fabulous Invalid, The American Way, The Cocoanuts,
Animal Crackers, First Lady,* and *Of Thee I Sing.* Admittedly some of
Kaufman's scripts should remain forgotten by everyone except theater
historians, but the repertoire of nearly twenty plays mentioned above
are uniquely American. These entertainments illustrate the evolution
that took place in our nation's drama, sense of humor, and history
during the first half of the twentieth century.

Our inheritance from George S. Kaufman is his views on the social,
political, financial, and theatrical pulse rate of the United States
through several decades. He holds up details of daily life for audience
scrutiny. He recognized and identified societal aberrations without offering fast, easy remedies. He was a reporter who did not believe
speedy solutions solved complex problems. One learns from Kaufman's
works that the quick fix may help for the moment; however, the real
dilemma continues to be hiding below the surface.

Our inheritance from George S. Kaufman is his style of witty, satirical comedy. With the Kaufman school of comedy, there remains the
inspiration he provided for countless dramatists. The George S. Kaufman legacy is a richly faceted American gemstone.

Notes and References

Chapter One

1. There are three biographies about Kaufman from which the basic factual information for this book has been taken. Howard Teichmann, *George S. Kaufman: An Intimate Portrait* (New York: Atheneum, 1972); Scott Meredith, *George S. Kaufman and his Friends* (Garden City, N.Y.: Doubleday, 1974); and Malcolm Goldstein, *George S. Kaufman: His Life, His Theatre* (New York: Oxford University Press, 1979).

2. John Geoffrey Hartman, *The Development of American Social Comedy From 1787 to 1936* (Philadelphia, n.p., 1939), 29–34.

3. In addition to the account retold in each biography, the first public account was written by Alexander Woollcott, "Profiles: The Deep, Tangled Kaufman," *New Yorker* (18 May 1929), 26. Woollcott had worked for Munsey from 1922 to 1928; he mischievously, but delicately retold the tale in print. Several years later Kaufman recounted a less revealing outline of the incident, which as Goldstein suggests in his book, *George S. Kaufman* (24), makes a joke of the situation. For Kaufman's version see Dilly Tante, ed., *Living Authors: A Book of Biographies* (New York: H. W. Wilson Co., 1932), 204.

4. This spelling of Seligman is taken from the manuscript of the play in the Library of Congress. Goldstein, *George S. Kaufman* (26), spells this name with a double *n*—Seligmann.

5. Goldstein, *George S. Kaufman,* 28.

6. "W. W. De Renne" taken from the play manuscript in the Library of Congress. Goldstein, *George S. Kaufman* (29), cites the name as "Wymberley de Renne."

7. Jamison is used for a number of characters in plays by Kaufman—as a surname in *The Cocoanuts,* 1925; *The Still Alarm,* 1929; *The Fabulous Invalid,* 1938; and as a single name in *Animal Crackers,* 1928.

8. This is another name that appears in a number of variations: Hans Mueller, Henry Miller, and Hans Miller.

9. *Variety* (14 November 1919), 18.

10. Sources for information on the Algonquin set: Frank Case, *Tales of a Wayward Inn* (New York: Frederick A. Stokes Co., 1938); Margaret Case Harriman, *The Vicious Circle: The Story of the Algonquin Round Table* (New York: Rinehart, 1951); and James R. Gaines, *Wit's End: Days and Nights of the Algonquin Round Table* (New York: Harcourt Brace Jovanovich, 1977).

Chapter Two

1. Paul T. Nolan, *Marc Connelly* (New York: Twayne Publishers, 1969), 26.
2. Marc Connelly, *Voices Offstage: A Book of Memoirs* (Chicago: Holt, Rinehart & Winston, 1968), 58.
3. Ibid., 59–60.
4. Arthur Hobson Quinn, *Contemporary American Plays* (New York: Charles Scribner's Sons, 1923), xxi.
5. Ibid., 76.
6. Harriman, *The Vicious Circle,* 43.
7. Ibid., 89.
8. Manuscript in the Library of Congress. Nonnumbered page also contains a list of characters; this page should follow title sheet.
9. Woollcott, "Profiles," 26.
10. Goldstein, *George S. Kaufman,* 86–87.
11. Connelly, *Voices Offstage,* 79.
12. Ibid., 79.
13. Goldstein, *George S. Kaufman,* 87.
14. Connelly, *Voices Offstage,* 105.
15. *New York Times,* "Review," 4 September 1924.
16. Connelly, *Voices Offstage,* 118.
17. Ibid.
18. John Corbin, *New York Times,* 17 February 1924, sec. 7, 1.
19. Clipping without a newspaper's name found in George S. Kaufman scrapbook inventoried as *George S. Kaufman Papers, Clippings, and Reviews: 1918–1932,* vol. 3, in Wisconsin Historical Society Library, Madison, Wisc. Hereafter cited as Kaufman, *Papers.*
20. Barrett Clark and George Freedley, *A History of Modern Drama* (New York: Appleton-Century-Crofts, 1947), 733.
21. Joseph Mersand, *Three Plays About Business in America* (New York: Washington Square Press, 1964), 89.
22. Connelly, *Voices Offstage,* 122.
23. Teichmann, *George S. Kaufman,* 86.
24. Goldstein, *George S. Kaufman,* 112.
25. Connelly, *Voices Offstage,* 123.

Chapter Three

1. Goldstein, *George S. Kaufman,* 93.
2. Ibid., 97.
3. Ibid., 120.
4. Ibid., 123.
5. Hector Arce, *Groucho* (New York: Putnam's Sons, 1979), 133–34.

6. Teichmann, *George S. Kaufman*, 92–93.

7. Goldstein, *George S. Kaufman*, 129.

8. Teichmann, *George S. Kaufman*, 91.

9. Ibid., 92.

10. Edna Ferber, *A Peculiar Treasure* (New York: Doubleday, Doran & Co., 1939), 284.

11. Goldstein, *George S. Kaufman*, 107.

12. Connelly, *Voices Offstage*, 60.

13. Ferber, *A Peculiar Treasure*, 288.

14. Ibid., 311.

15. Ibid., 312.

16. Goldstein, *George S. Kaufman*, 140.

17. Ibid., 138.

18. Corey Ford, *The Time of Laughter* (Boston: Little, Brown & Co., 1967), 104–5.

19. Laurence Shyer, "American Absurd: Two Nonsense Plays by George S. Kaufman and Morrie Ryskind, and Ring Lardner," *Theatre*, Spring, 1978, 119–24. The script of *Something New* is published as part of the article.

20. Donald Elder, *Ring Lardner* (Garden City, N.Y.: Doubleday, 1956), 277.

21. Clipping without a newspaper's name found in George S. Kaufman's scrapbook inventoried as Kaufman, *Papers*, vol. 3.

22. Joseph Wood Krutch, *The American Drama Since 1918: An Informal History* (New York: George Braziller, 1957), 140.

23. As cited in Edwin P. Hoyt, *Alexander Woollcott: The Man Who Came to Dinner* (London: Abelard-Schuman, 1968), 205.

Chapter Four

1. Harriman, *The Vicious Circle*, 288.

2. Max Gordon with Lewis Funke, *Max Gordon Presents* (New York: Bernard Geis Associates, 1963, 157–65) is a recount of the "Flying Colors" events from Gordon's perspective.

3. Goldstein, *George S. Kaufman*, 197–99.

4. Clark and Freedley, *A History of Modern Drama*, 736.

5. Clipping without additional information found in Kaufman, *Papers*, vol. 3.

6. Ibid.

7. Ibid.

8. Eleanor Flexner, *American Playwrights 1918-1938*, (Freeport, N.Y.: Books for Libraries Press, 1966) 221.

9. Ibid.

10. Clipping without a date in Kaufman, *Papers*, vol. 3.

11. Clipping without a date or newspaper title in Kaufman, *Papers,* vol. 3.

12. Ferber, *A Peculiar Treasure,* 387.

13. Ibid.

Chapter Five

1. Moss Hart, "Men at Work," *Six Plays By Kaufman and Hart* (New York: Modern Library, Random House, 1942), xxii.

2. Moss Hart, *Act One: An Autobiography* (New York: Random House, 1959), 392.

3. Flexner, *American Playwrights,* 216.

4. Hart, *Act One,* 427.

5. Flexner, *American Playwrights,* 223–24; John Howard Lawson, *Theory and Technique of Playwriting* (New York: Hill & Wang, 1980 reprint), 257–60.

6. Goldstein, *George S. Kaufman,* 232.

7. Flexner, *American Playwrights,* 225.

8. Brooks Atkinson, "Introduction," *Six Plays By Kaufman and Hart,* xv–xvi.

9. Krutch, *American Drama Since 1918,* 148.

10. Goldstein, *George S. Kaufman,* 308.

11. Clipping without a date found in Kaufman, *Papers,* vol. 4.

12. Goldstein, *George S. Kaufman,* 335.

13. Robert Rice, "Rice and Old Shoes," *PM,* 3 February 1941, 22; as cited in Goldstein, *George S. Kaufman,* 479 n.48.

Chapter Six

1. Edna Ferber, *A Kind of Magic* (Garden City, N.Y.: Doubleday, 1963), 132.

2. Goldstein, *George S. Kaufman,* 354.

3. Ferber, *A Kind of Magic,* 137.

4. Gordon, *Max Gordon Presents,* 242.

5. Ibid., 243.

6. Ferber, *A Kind of Magic,* 137.

7. Ibid.

8. Meredith, *George S. Kaufman and his Friends,* 592.

9. Ferber, *A Kind of Magic,* 239.

10. Ibid., 240.

Chapter Seven

1. Gordon, *Max Gordon Presents,* 298.

2. Teichmann, *George S. Kaufman,* 338.

3. Abe Burrows, *Honest, Abe, Is there Really No Business Like Show Business?* (Boston: Little, Brown & Co., 1980), 273.

4. Goldstein, *George S. Kaufman,* 448.

5. Gordon, *Max Gordon Presents,* 246.

Selected Bibliography

PRIMARY SOURCES

The plays—full length and sketches—are listed by the year in which they were written with the date of the first New York performance in parentheses. The publisher or a manuscript location is listed according to the availability at the time when the research for this book was undertaken.

1. Plays
"The Failure," with Irving Pichael, 1911. Manuscript Division, Library of Congress.
"The Lunatic," with Herbert Seligman, 1914. Manuscript Division, Library of Congress.
"That Infernal Machine," with W. W. De Renne. 1915. Manuscript Division, Library of Congress.
"Going Up!" 1917. Manuscript Division, Library of Congress.
"Someone in the House," with Walter C. Percival. 1918. Theatre Collection, New York Public Library.
"Third Man High," with Robert Nathan. 1919. Manuscript Division, Library of Congress.
"Duval, M.D." 1919. George Crouse Tyler Papers, Princeton University.
Dulcy, with Marc Connelly, New York: G. P. Putnam's Sons, 1921. New York: Samuel French, 1923. (13 August 1921)
To The Ladies!, with Marc Connelly. In *Contemporary American Plays,* edited by Arthur Hobson Quinn. New York: Charles Scribner's Sons, 1923. (20 February 1922)
"Big Casino Is Little Casino," sketch from "No Siree!" (revue). 1922. Manuscript Division, Library of Congress. (30 April 1922)
"Life in the Back Pages," sketch from "The 49ers" (revue). 1922. George Crouse Tyler Papers, Princeton University. (7 November 1922).
Merton of the Movies, with Marc Connelly. New York: Samuel French, 1925. (13 November 1922)
A Christmas Carol, with Marc Connelly. *The Bookman* 56, December 1922: 409–419.
"Helen of Troy, New York," with Marc Connelly. Music and lyrics by Bert

Kalmar and Harry Ruby. 1923. Manuscript Division, Library of Congress. (19 June 1923)

If Men Played Cards as Women Do, sketch from "Third Music Box Revue." In *The Greatest Revue Sketches,* edited by Donald Oliver. New York: Avon Books, 1982. (22 September 1923)

"The Deep Tangled Wildwood," with Marc Connelly. (Various titles: "West of Pittsburgh" (1922), "The Old Home Town" (1923), "Little Old Millersville.") Theatre Collection, New York Public Library. (5 November 1923)

Beggar on Horseback, with Marc Connelly. In *Twenty-Five Best Plays of Modern American Theatre,* edited by John Gassner. New York: Crown Publishers, 1967. (12 February 1924)

"Wayward Bound," with Isabel Leighton. 1924. Manuscript Division, Library of Congress.

"Beggar off Horseback," sketch from "'Round the Town" (revue), with Marc Connelly, Manuscript Division, Library of Congress. (21 May 1924)

"Be Yourself," with Marc Connelly, Music and lyrics by Lewis Gensler and Milton Schwarzwald, additional lyrics by Ira Gershwin. No known extant manuscript. (3 September 1924)

Minick, with Edna Ferber. New York: Samuel French, 1925. (24 September 1924)

The Butter and Egg Man. New York: Samuel French, 1930. (25 September 1925)

"Nothing Coming In," with Herman J. Mankiewicz, 1925. Manuscript Division, Library of Congress.

The Cocoanuts. Music and lyrics by Irving Berlin. In *By George: A Kaufman Collection,* edited by Donald Oliver. New York: St. Martin's Press, 1979. (8 December 1925)

The Good Fellow, with Herman J. Mankiewicz. New York: Samuel French, 1926. (5 October 1926)

"Shop Talk." Sketch from annual show of the Dutch Treat Club. Manuscript Division, Library of Congress. (1926)

The Royal Family, with Edna Ferber. Garden City, N.Y.: Nelson Doubleday, 1976; New York: Samuel French, 1976. (28 December 1927)

"Strike Up the Band." Music and lyrics by George and Ira Gershwin. 1927. Anne Kaufman Schneider (private Collection). (The production staged on Broadway 14 January 1930 was not revised by Kaufman.)

Animal Crackers, with Morrie Ryskind. Music and lyrics by Bert Kalmar and Harry Ruby. New York: Samuel French, 1929, 1984. 1928 manuscript in Theatre Collection, Princeton University. (23 October 1928)

The Still Alarm, sketch from "The Little Show." In *The Greatest Revue Sketches,* edited by Donald Oliver, 1982. (30 April 1929)

June Moon, with Ring Lardner. *George S. Kaufman and his Collaborators.* New
    York: Performing Arts Journal Publications, 1984. (9 October 1929)
"The Channel Road," with Alexander Woollcott. Manuscript Division, Li-
    brary of Congress. (17 October 1929)
Something New, with Morrie Ryskind. 1929. In Laurence Shyer "American
    Absurd: Two Nonsense Plays by George S. Kaufman and Morrie Ryskind,
    and Ring Lardner," *Theatre,* Spring 1978, 119-24.
Once in a Lifetime, with Moss Hart. *Six Plays by Kaufman and Hart.* New York:
    Modern Library, Random House, 1942. (24 September 1930)
"The Band Wagon," with Howard Dietz. The Walter Hampden-Edwin Booth
    Theatre Collection and Library at The Players, New York City. (3 June
    1931)
Of Thee I Sing, with Morrie Ryskind. Music by George Gershwin and lyrics
    by Ira Gershwin. New York: Samuel French, 1935. (December 26, 1931)
Dinner at Eight, with Edna Ferber, New York: Samuel French, 1935. (22
    October 1932)
"Service," sketch for the Dutch Treat Club Annual Revue, with Marc Con-
    nelly. 1932. The Walter Hampden-Edwin Booth Theatre Collection and
    Library, New York City.
On the American Plan, sketch for "Flying Colors," with Howard Dietz. In *The
    Greatest Revue Sketches,* edited by Donald Oliver, 1982. (15 September
    1932)
Let 'Em Eat Cake, with Morrie Ryskind. Music by George Gershwin and lyrics
    by Ira Gershwin. New York: Alfred A. Knopf, 1933. (21 October 1933)
The Dark Tower, with Alexander Woollcott. New York: Random House,
    1934. (25 November 1933)
Merrily We Roll Along, with Moss Hart. *Six Plays by Kaufman and Hart.* New
    York: Modern Library, 1942. (29 September 1934)
"Bring On the Girls," with Morrie Ryskind. Manuscript Division, Library of
    Congress. (22 October 1934)
First Lady, with Katherine Dayton. New York: Dramatist Play Service, 1936.
    (26 November 1935)
Stage Door, with Edna Ferber. New York: Dramatist Play Service, 1936. (22
    October 1936)
You Can't Take It with You, with Moss Hart. *Six Plays by Kaufman and Hart.*
    New York: Modern Library, 1942. (14 December 1936)
Meet the Audience. 1936. Manuscript Division, Library of Congress. In *By
    George,* compiled by Donald Oliver. New York: St. Martin's Press, 1979.
I'd Rather Be Right, with Moss Hart. Music by Richard Rogers and lyrics by
    Lorenz Hart. New York: Random House, 1937. (2 November 1937)
The Fabulous Invalid, with Moss Hart. New York: Random House, 1938. (8
    October 1938)
Gone with the Revolution, sketch for "Sing Out the News," with Moss Hart. In

The Greatest Revue Sketches, edited by Donald Oliver. New York: Avon Books, 1982. (24 September 1938)

The American Way, with Moss Hart. *Six Plays by Kaufman and Hart.* New York: Modern Library, 1942. (21 January 1939)

The Man Who Came to Dinner, with Moss Hart. *Six Plays by Kaufman and Hart.* New York: Modern Library, 1942. (16 October 1939)

George Washington Slept Here, with Moss Hart. *Six Plays by Kaufman and Hart.* New York: Modern Library 1942. (18 October 1940)

The Land Is Bright, with Edna Ferber. New York: Dramatist Play Service, 1941. (28 October 1941)

Dream On, Soldier, with Moss Hart. *Theatre Arts* vol. xxvli, no. 9, September 1943: 533–35.

The Late George Apley, with John P. Marquand. *George S. Kaufman and his Collaborators.* New York: Performing Arts Journal Publications, 1984. (21 November 1944)

Local Boy Makes Good, sketch for "The Seven Lively Arts." In *The Greatest Revue Sketches,* edited by Donald Oliver. New York: Avon Books, 1982. (7 December 1944)

Hollywood Pinafore or The Lad Who Loved A Salary. The Walter Hampden-Edwin Booth Theatre Collection. (31 May 1945) In *By George,* compiled by Donald Oliver. New York: St. Martin's Press, 1979.

Park Avenue, with Nunnally Johnson. Music by Arthur Schwartz and lyrics by Ira Gershwin. Anne Kaufman Schneider Collection. (4 November 1946)

Bravo, with Edna Ferber. *George S. Kaufman and his Collaborators.* New York: Performing Arts Journal Publications, 1984. (11 November 1944)

The Small Hours, with Leueen MacGrath. New York: Dramatists Play Service, 1951. (15 February 1951)

Fancy Meeting You Again, with Leueen MacGrath, New York: Dramatists Play Service, 1952. (14 January 1952)

The Solid Gold Cadillac, with Howard Teichmann. 1954. New York: Dramatists Play Service, 1954. (5 November 1953)

"In the Money," with Howard Teichmann. 1954. Wisconsin Center for Film and Theatre Research, Madison.

"Exile," with Howard Teichmann. 1954. Wisconsin Center for Film and Theatre Research, Madison.

Silk Stockings, with Leueen MacGrath plus Abe Burrows, Music and lyrics by Cole Porter. New York: Tams-Witmark Music Library, 1955. (24 February 1955)

"The Lipstick War," with Alan Campbell. 1956. Wisconsin Center for Film and Theatre Research, Madison.

Amicable Parting, with Leueen MacGrath. 1957. New York: Dramatists Play Service, 1957.

"The Same as Before Only Worse," with Ruth Goetz. Music by Cy Coleman and lyrics by Carolyn Leigh. 1958. Wisconsin Center for Film and Theatre Research, Madison.
"I Give It Six Months," with Leueen MacGrath. 1959. Wisconsin Center for Film and Theatre Research, Madison.

2. Films

Roman Scandals, with Robert E. Sherwood. 1933. Film still available.
A Night at the Opera, with Morrie Ryskind. 1935. New York: A Viking Film Book, 1972.
"Sleeper Jump," with Herman J. Mankiewicz. 1942. Wisconsin Center for Film and Theatre Research, Madison.
"And Baby Makes Two," with Leueen MacGrath. 1952. Wisconsin Center for Film and Theatre Research, Madison.
"The Hat," with Leueen MacGrath. A play for television. 1953. Wisconsin Center for Film and Theatre Research, Madison.

3. Miscellaneous

George S. Kaufman and His Collaborators. New York: Performing Arts Journal Publications, 1984.
Six Plays By Kaufman and Hart. Introduction by Brooks Atkinson. New York: Modern Library, Random House, 1942.
Three Plays by Kaufman and Hart. New York: Grove Press, 1980.
By George: A Kaufman Collection. Compiled and edited by Donald Oliver. New York: St. Martin's Press, 1979.

SECONDARY SOURCES

Atkinson, Brooks. *Broadway.* New York: MacMillan Publishing Co., 1974. Interesting history with many references to Kaufman.
Burrows, Abe. *Honest, Abe: Is There Really No Business Like Show Business?* Boston: Little, Brown & Co., 1980. Excellent segments on Burrows' 1950s working relationship with Kaufman.
Case, Frank. *Tales of a Wayward Inn.* New York: Frederick A. Stokes Co., 1938. Personal account of the Algonquin Round Table by the proprietor of the Algonquin Hotel.
Chatterton, Wayne. *Alexander Woollcott.* TUSAS 305. Boston: Twayne Publishers, 1978. Helpful reference for gaining an understanding of Woollcott.

Clark, Barrett H., and Freedley, George. *A History Of Modern Drama.* New York: Appleton-Century-Crofts, 1947. A reference book that includes segments on Kaufman that place his work in a 1940s perspective.

Connelly, Marc. *Voices Offstage: A Book of Memoirs.* Chicago: Holt, Rinehart & Winston, 1968. Connelly's remembrances of his collaborations with Kaufman—facts not always reliable.

Dickinson, Thomas H. *Playwrights of the American Theater.* New York: Macmillan Co., 1925. Opinion of Kaufman's work and position in American drama as seen in mid-twenties.

Ferber, Edna. *A Peculiar Treasure.* New York: Doubleday, Doran & Co., 1939. Detailed discussions regarding collaborations with Kaufman from *Minick* (1924) through *Stage Door* (1936).

————. *A Kind of Magic.* Garden City, N.Y.: Doubleday & Co., 1963. Personal accounts of working with Kaufman on *The Land is Bright* and *Bravo!*

Flexner, Eleanor. *American Playwrights: 1918-1938. The Theatre Retreats from Reality.* Freeport, N.Y.: Books for Libraries Press, 1966 reprint. Chapter on comedy includes opinions of Kaufman's plays.

Ford, Corey. *The Time of Laughter.* Boston: Little, Brown & Co., 1967. An excellent account of the "Algonquin Wits" and their era. Written by a younger member of the group.

Gaines, James R. *Wit's End: Days and Nights of the Algonquin Round Table.* New York: Harcourt Brace Jovanovich, 1977. An interpretive biographical essay about the Round Tablers focusing on specific persons (including Kaufman), who played the most significant roles in the group's social, cultural, and literary efforts.

Gilbert, Julie Goldsmith. *Ferber: A Biography.* Garden City, N.Y.: Doubleday & Co., 1978. Interesting account of Ferber's life written by her great-niece; many references to Kaufman.

Goldstein, Malcolm. *George S. Kaufman: His Life, His Theater.* New York: Oxford University Press, 1979. An excellent, reliable biography with critical evaluations of the plays.

Harriman, Margaret Case. *The Vicious Circle: The Story of the Algonquin Round Table.* New York: Rinehart & Co., 1951. The daughter of Frank Case, proprietor of the hotel, writes a complete, reliable account of the development and disintegration of the Algonquin Round Table.

Hart, Moss. *Act One: An Autobiography.* New York: Random House, 1959. Part 2 recounts events surrounding the evolution of *Once in a Lifetime.*

Hartman, John Geoffrey. *The Development of American Social Comedy from 1787 to 1936.* Philadelphia: no publisher indicated, 1939. Introduction to American social comedy from 1787 to 1936.

Krutch, Joseph Wood. *The American Drama since 1918: An Informal History.* New York: George Braziller, 1957. Critical evaluation of playwriting in America from World War I to 1957.

Mantle, Burns. *American Playwrights of Today.* New York: Dodd, Mead & Co., 1929. Evaluation of playwrights of the 1920s including Kaufman.

Meredith, Scott. *George S. Kaufman and His Friends.* Garden City, N.Y.: Doubleday & Co., 1974. Detailed biography.

Mersand, Joseph. *The American Drama: 1930–1940.* New York: Modern Chapbooks, 1941. Another general assessment of plays and playwrights of a particular period including Kaufman.

Nolan, Paul T. *Marc Connelly.* TUSAS 149. New York: Twayne Publishers, 1969. A chapter devoted to the collaborations with Kaufman plus other scattered references.

Quinn, Arthur Hobson. *A History of the American Drama: From the Civil War to the Present Day.* New York: Appleton-Century-Crofts, 1936. A good general survey of American drama with insightful material on Kaufman.

Teichmann, Howard. *George S. Kaufman: An Intimate Portrait.* New York: Atheneum, 1972. A personal account of his relationship with Kaufman and many fascinating anecdotes.

————. *Smart Aleck: The Wit, World, and Life of Alexander Woollcott.* New York: William Morrow & Co., 1976. Numerous Kaufman entries and an interesting chapter about *The Man Who Came to Dinner.*

Index